EPHESIANS

OUR RICHES IN CHRIST

AT A GLANCE

Serendipity House / P.O. Box 1012 / Littleton, CO 80160

TOLL FREE 1-800-525-9563 / www.serendipityhouse.com

00 01 / **301 series • CHG** / 4 3 2

PROJECT ENGINEER:
Lyman Coleman

WRITING TEAM:
Richard Peace, Lyman Coleman, Andrew Sloan, Cathy Tardif

PRODUCTION TEAM:
Christopher Werner, Sharon Penington, Erika Tiepel

COVER PHOTO:
© 1998 Ron Watts / Westlight

CORE VALUES

Community:	The purpose of this curriculum is to build community within the body of believers around Jesus Christ.
Group Process:	To build community, the curriculum must be designed to take a group through a step-by-step process of sharing your story with one another.
Interactive Bible Study:	To share your "story," the approach to Scripture in the curriculum needs to be open-ended and right brain—to "level the playing field" and encourage everyone to share.
Developmental Stages:	To provide a healthy program in the life cycle of a group, the curriculum needs to offer courses on three levels of commitment: (1) Beginner Stage—low-level entry, high structure, to level the playing field; (2) Growth Stage—deeper Bible study, flexible structure, to encourage group accountability; (3) Discipleship Stage—in-depth Bible study, open structure, to move the group into high gear.
Target Audiences:	To build community throughout the culture of the church, the curriculum needs to be flexible, adaptable and transferable into the structure of the average church.

ACKNOWLEDGMENTS

To Zondervan Bible Publishers
for permission to use
the NIV text,
The Holy Bible, New International Bible Society.
© 1973, 1978, 1984 by International Bible Society.
Used by permission of Zondervan Bible Publishers.

WELCOME TO THE SERENDIPITY 301 DEPTH BIBLE STUDY SERIES

You are about to embark on an adventure into the powerful experience of depth Bible Study. The Serendipity 301 series combines three basic elements to produce a life-changing and group-changing course.

First, you will be challenged and enriched by the personal Bible Study that begins each unit. You will have the opportunity to dig into Scripture both for understanding and personal reflection. Although some groups may choose to do this section together at their meeting, doing it beforehand will greatly add to the experience of the course.

Second, you will benefit from the group sessions. Wonderful things happen when a small group of people get together and share their lives around the Word of God. Not only will you have a chance to take your personal study to a deeper level, you will have an opportunity to share on a deep level what's happening in your life and receive the encouragement and prayer support of your group.

Third, the 301 courses provide the stimulus and tools for your group to take steps toward fulfilling your group mission. Whether or not your group has gone through the preparation of a Serendipity 101 and 201 course, you can profit from this mission emphasis. The 32-page center section of this book will guide you through this process. And questions in the closing section of the group agenda will prompt your group to act upon the mission challenge to "give birth" to a new small group.

Put these three components together, and you have a journey in Christian discipleship well worth the effort. Enjoy God's Word! Enjoy genuine Christian community! Enjoy dreaming about your mission!

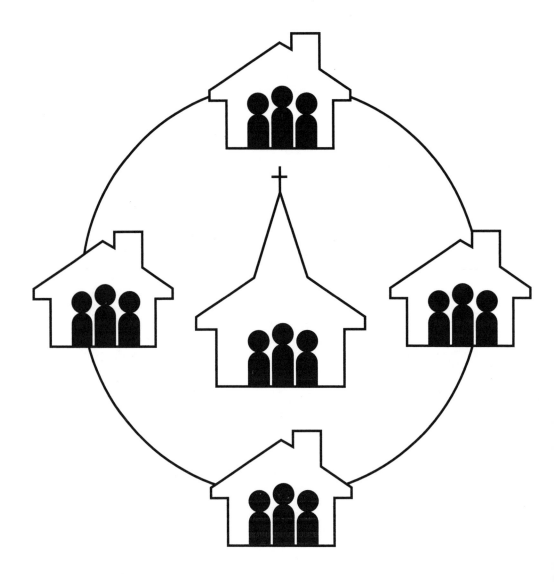

QUESTIONS & ANSWERS

STAGE

1. What stage in the life cycle of a small group is this course designed for?

Turn to the first page of the center section of this book. There you will see that this 301 course is designed for the third stage of a small group. In the Serendipity "Game Plan" for the multiplication of small groups, your group is in the Release Stage.

GOALS

2. What are the goals of a 301 study course?

As shown on the second page of the center section (page M2), the focus in this third stage is heavy on Bible Study and Mission.

BIBLE STUDY

3. What is the approach to Bible Study in this course?

This course involves two types of Bible Study. The "homework" assignment fosters growth in personal Bible study skills and in personal spiritual growth. The group study gives everyone a chance to share their learning and together take it to a deeper level.

SELF STUDY

4. What does the homework involve?

There are three parts to each assignment: (1) READ—to get the "bird's-eye view" of the passage and record your first impressions; (2) SEARCH—to get the "worm's-eye view" by digging into the passage verse-by-verse with specific questions; and (3) APPLY—to ask yourself, after studying the passage, "What am I going to do about it?"

THREE-STAGE LIFE CYCLE OF A GROUP

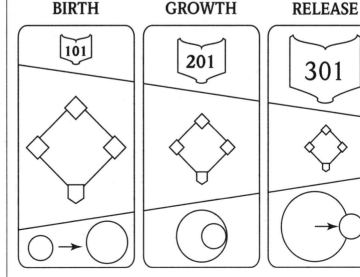

BIBLE KNOWLEDGE

5. *What if you don't know very much about the Bible?*

No problem. The homework assignment is designed to lead you step-by-step in your study. And there are study notes in each unit to give you help with key words, concepts and difficult passages.

AGENDA

6. *What is the agenda for the group meetings?*

The completed homework assignment becomes the basis for the group sharing. (However, those who don't do the homework should definitely be encouraged to come to the meeting anyway.) During the meeting the group will be guided to share on three levels: (1) TO BEGIN; (2) TO GO DEEPER; and (3) TO CLOSE.

STAYING ON TRACK

7. *How can the group get through all the material?*

Following the recommended time limits for each of the three sections will help keep you on track. Since you may not be able to answer all the questions with the time you have, you may need to skip some of them. Also, if you have more than seven people at a meeting, use the "Fearless Foursomes" described below for the Bible Study.

THE FEARLESS FOURSOME!

If you have more than seven people at a meeting, Serendipity recommends you divide into groups of 4 for the Bible Study. Count off around the group: "one, two, one, two, etc."—and have the "ones" move quickly to another room for the Bible Study. Ask one person to be the leader and follow the directions for the Bible Study time. After 30 minutes, the Group Leader will call "Time" and ask all groups to come together for the Caring Time.

GROUP BUILDING

8. *How does this course develop Group Building?*

Although this series is Serendipity's deepest Bible Study curriculum, Group Building is still essential. The group will continue "checking in" with each other and will challenge each other to grow in Christian discipleship. Working together on the group's mission should also be a very positive group-building process.

**MISSION /
MULTIPLICATION**

9. *What is the mission of a 301 group?*

Page M3 of the center section summarizes the mission of groups using this course: to commission a team from your group to start a new group. The center section will lead your group in doing this.

**LEADERSHIP
TRAINING**

10. *How do we incorporate this mission into the course?*

Page M5 of the center section gives an overview of the six steps in this process. You can either add this leadership training to the sessions a little bit at a time or in a couple of separate sessions.

**GROUP
COVENANT**

11. *What is a group covenant?*

A group covenant is a "contract" that spells out your expectations and the ground rules for your group. It's very important that your group discuss these issues—preferably as part of the first session (also see page M32 in the center section).

**GROUND
RULES**

12. *What are the ground rules for the group?* (Check those that you agree upon.)

❑ PRIORITY: While you are in the course, you give the group meetings priority.

❑ PARTICIPATION: Everyone participates and no one dominates.

❑ RESPECT: Everyone is given the right to their own opinion and all questions are encouraged and respected.

❑ CONFIDENTIALITY: Anything that is said in the meeting is never repeated outside the meeting.

❑ EMPTY CHAIR: The group stays open to new people at every meeting as long as they understand the ground rules.

❑ SUPPORT: Permission is given to call upon each other in time of need—even in the middle of the night.

❑ ADVICE GIVING: Unsolicited advice is not allowed.

❑ MISSION: We agree to do everything in our power to start a new group as our mission (see center section).

INTRODUCTION TO THE BOOK OF EPHESIANS

The respected commentator, William Barclay, called Ephesians "The Queen of the Epistles." Samuel Taylor Coleridge, the English poet, said it was "the divinest composition of man." Armitage Robinson, who wrote a great commentary on this book, concluded that it was "the crown of St. Paul's writings." Indeed, there is a breathtaking grandeur about Paul's letter to the Ephesians, sketching as it does the reconciling work of God in Christ which makes one all the peoples of the earth; by which the hostile cosmic powers are subdued; and through which a new humanity and a new society are created. It is with much awe that one approaches Ephesians, the "greatest" and "most relevant for us" of all Paul's epistles (John Mackay).

The Prison Epistles

The letter to the Ephesians is one of four letters known as the Prison Epistles. It was written when Paul was (once again) in jail. Epaphras has come to visit him there, bearing disturbing news about the church at Colosse. Apparently, heretical teaching had begun to take root in the church, threatening its very existence. So Paul writes the Christians at Colosse (the letter to the Colossians). He also writes a private letter to one of the members of the church there, Philemon. A slave by the name of Onesimus, owned by Philemon, has been converted through Paul's ministry and is now returning to his master, all of which is explained by Paul in the letter to Philemon. The third letter (Ephesians) is written to neighboring churches in the Roman province of Asia (see map). All three letters were delivered by Tychicus, Paul's "dear brother and faithful servant in the Lord" (6:21). The fourth Prison Epistle, Philippians, was written on a different occasion.

Relationship to Colossians

Ephesians and Colossians are very much alike—so much so that 75 of the 155 verses in Ephesians are found in parallel form in Colossians. There are more similarities between Ephesians and Colossians than between any other two New Testament books. (This fact is made even more remarkable in the light of the close ties between Matthew, Mark and Luke.) How did this come about?

A close comparison of the two letters shows that what we have here is not simply a matter of parts of one letter being copied into parts of the other letter. The parallel is more in terms of *thought* and *expression.* For example, we find the same phrases in both letters. In both Ephesians 5:16 and Colossians 4:5 Paul speaks about "making the most of every opportunity" ("redeeming the time" as the KJV eloquently puts it); in Ephesians 4:2 and Colossians 3:13 he urges us to "bear with one another"; in Ephesians 3:17 and Colossians 2:7 Paul speaks about being "rooted and established in love." None of these phrases is used elsewhere by Paul. For other examples of parallel phrases, see also Ephesians 1:23; 3:19; 4:13 and Colossians 1:19; 2:9, Ephesians 2:12; 4:18 and Colossians 1:21; Ephesians 1:7 and Colossians 1:14; Ephesians 1:13 and Colossians 1:5; Ephesians 5:5 and Colossians 3:5; Ephesians 4:16 and Colossians 2:19.

There is also a parallel in theme. In both letters, Paul addresses the theme of the relationship between husband and wife; parents and child; slave and master (Eph. 5:21–6:9 and Col. 3:18–4:1). In both letters, Christian living is discussed in terms of putting off the old man and putting on the new (Eph. 4:17–32 and Col. 3:5–14). In both letters, we find the injunction to express thanks via hymns and songs (Eph. 5:15–20 and Col. 3:16–17). For further examples of parallel themes, see Ephesians 1:15ff and Colossians 1:3ff; Ephesians 6:18–20 and Colossians 4:3–6; Ephesians 3:1–13 and Colossians 1:23–29.

How did these two letters come to be similar? The best guess is that Paul first dealt with these themes in his letter to the Colossians, written to address the Colossian heresy. His letter to them was intended to be the antidote to the false teaching they were embracing. But then Paul began to ponder what he had said and was captivated by the truth and the majesty of it all. What was true in a local situation, was also true in all situations. The specifics in Colossians are then cast into universals in Ephesians.

Destination

There is good reason to believe that Ephesians was not written solely for the church (or churches) at Ephesus, but rather was a circular letter intended to be read by all the churches in Asia Minor. For one thing, the phrase "in Ephesus" is not found in several of the very early and major Greek manuscripts. They simply read: "Paul, an apostle of Jesus Christ by the will of God, to the faithful in Christ Jesus." For another thing, Ephesians is curiously impersonal for someone who spent years in Ephesus as Paul did (see Acts 18:19–21; 19:1–20; 20:1,13–37). There are no greetings (by contrast, 26 people are greeted in Romans 16, and Paul had yet to visit that church!). The tone is neutral. There are no intimate asides shared with friends; no remembrances of common experiences. In fact, Ephesians is Paul's most impersonal letter. This would hardly have been the case were he writing just to his many friends in Ephesus. Finally, the letter itself seems to suggest that Paul and the recipients did not know one another. In 1:15 Paul says, "ever since I heard about your faith ... ." In 3:2 he writes, "Surely you have heard about the administration of God's grace that was given to me for you ..." (see also 4:21).

Some have suggested that Ephesians is actually the lost letter to the Laodiceans (Col. 4:16); or that it was addressed to newly converted Gentile Christians in Ephesus not known to Paul. But the best guess seems to be that this was a circular letter carried by Tychicus and read at each stop he made in Asia Minor—finally ending up in Ephesus, the capital city, where it assumed the name of the church there.

Place and Date of Writing

It is unclear from which city Paul wrote. It seems that he was in prisons throughout the empire (see 2 Cor. 11:23)! While Caesarea (Acts 24) and Ephesus have been suggested as possible sites, the most likely place was Rome (Acts 28), meaning that the letter to the Ephesians was written in the early 60s, some 30 years after Jesus' crucifixion and a few years before Paul's death.

Style

Ephesians is an unusual letter, stylistically, for Paul. When it is compared to his other letters, even in the English translation (and much more in the Greek original), it has a different "feel" to it. Paul uses new words here. In fact, there are more than 80 words in Ephesians not found elsewhere in his writings. Thirty-eight of his words do not occur anywhere else in the New Testament. Furthermore, Paul does *not* use words which we have come to associate with his writings such as "justify." Also, the sentences are longer in Ephesians (though this does not show up so clearly in the English translation.) Ephesians 1:3–14,15–23; 2:1–9 and 3:1–7 are each single sentences in Greek. There is a poetic, rhapsodic quality to Ephesians which is arresting and haunting. Ephesians is more a poem than prose. In fact, it is more a prayer than even a poem.

Because of these stylistic differences, some modern critics have questioned whether Paul actually wrote the letter (see note for 1:1). In fact, this argument is not very convincing since great writers (and certainly Paul was one) often write in different styles in accord with different purposes (compare Shakespeare's *Othello* with his *A Midsummer Night's Dream*). This was a different kind of letter for Paul. It was not dashed off in the midst of a busy ministry in order to deal with a pressing problem in a remote church. In actuality, this is a mature, reasoned reflection—written while he was in prison and had time for such meditation. Furthermore, in Ephesians Paul does not launch a new theme. He had just written Colossians. In dealing with the particular heresy they were facing, he sounded many of the themes later found in Ephesians. Ephesians is his reflection on the underlying realities upon which he based his specific answers to the local problems in Colosse.

Ephesians in reality is a meditation. The first three chapters are more a long prayer with several asides than anything else. And Paul's vocabulary and style are chosen with this intention in mind. Far from "proving" that Paul did not write Ephesians, the style of this short book proves what a superb writer, thinker and theologian Paul really was.

Outline

The emphasis throughout Ephesians is on unity. In chapters 1–3, Paul extols the great reconciling work of Christ, who through the Cross overcame the demonic powers (chapter 1) and thus broke down the wall between God and people (2:1–10) and the wall between Jew and Gentile (2:11–22). Then in chapters 4–6, Paul exhorts us to unity via a series of imperatives: We are to live out in our daily lives this unity which is a fact on a cosmic level.

In other words, as John Stott notes, the book of Ephesians moves from theory to practice; from doctrine to duty; from what God has done to what we are to do.

In between the introductory greetings (1:1–2) and the concluding salutation (6:21–24)—both typical of letters written in the first century—Paul's words fall into two distinct sections:

	Section One (Chapters 1–3)	Section Two (Chapters 4–6)
Focus:	Doctrine	Ethics
Style:	Preaching	Teaching
Topics:	The new life in a new society	The new standards and the new relationships
Tone:	Indicative (these are the facts of our new situation)	Imperative (this is what we must now do in the light of this new reality)
Concern:	The Christian faith	The Christian life

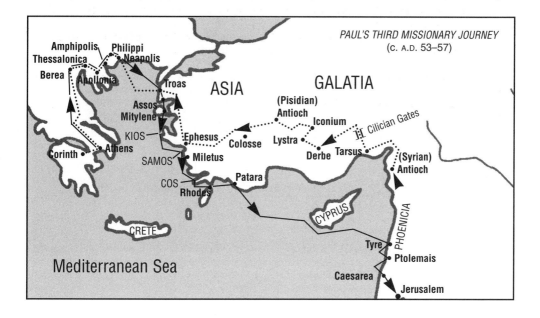

PAUL'S THIRD MISSIONARY JOURNEY
(C. A.D. 53–57)

Amphipolis, Philippi, Neapolis, Thessalonica, Berea, Apollonia, Troas, Assos, Mitylene, KIOS, Ephesus, Colosse, Corinth, Athens, SAMOS, Miletus, COS, Rhodes, Patara, CRETE, ASIA, GALATIA, (Pisidian) Antioch, Iconium, Lystra, Derbe, Tarsus, Cilician Gates, (Syrian) Antioch, CYPRUS, PHOENICIA, Tyre, Ptolemais, Caesarea, Jerusalem, Mediterranean Sea

UNIT 1—Salutation / Ephesians 1:1–2

1 **Paul, an apostle of Christ Jesus by the will of God,**
To the saints in Ephesus,ᵃ the faithfulᵇ in Christ Jesus:
   ²Grace and peace to you from God our Father and the Lord Jesus Christ.

[a]1 Some early manuscripts do not have *in Ephesus.*
[b]1 Or *believers who are*

READ

Two readings of the passage are suggested—each with a response to be checked or filled in on the worksheet.

First Reading / First Impressions: To get familiar with the passage as though you are reading this passage for the first time and to record your "first impressions" on the worksheet.

Read the first chapter (1:1–23) and check the box that best describes the style of this Scripture to you.
- ❐ warm, personal letter
- ❐ memo to employees
- ❐ formal, legal document
- ❐ affectionate, homey feeling
- ❐ heavy, theological tone
- ❐ locker-room pep talk

Second Reading / Big Idea: To get the overall idea, thought or "gist" of the passage, as though you are seeing the action from the press box—high above the stadium.

Read the first chapter again and check the box that best describes the "big idea" in the first chapter for you.
- ❐ You ought to be ashamed of yourself.
- ❐ I'm writing because I'm concerned for you.
- ❐ You can have it all in Christ.
- ❐ I'm proud of you.
- ❐ Get ready for a "chewing out."
- ❐ Let's get on with it.

SEARCH
1. Read Acts 19:8–41 and 20:17–38. List the facts you find about the church in Ephesus.

2. What do the terms Paul uses to describe himself in this letter—1:1; 3:1,7; 4:1; 6:20—show about him? How do you feel about seeing yourself in that way?

3. Read the note on the next page about "the saints." To what extent do you see yourself as a "saint"?

4. How would you define the titles Paul uses for Jesus to someone unfamiliar with these terms?

Christ (1:1)

Lord (1:2)

5. How has "grace and peace" (1:2) been an appropriate way to sum up the Gospel for you?

APPLY

As you begin this course, what are some goals you would like to work on? Check one or two from the list below and add another if you wish.

❏ to get to know God in a more personal way
❏ to understand what I believe as a Christian and where I stand on issues
❏ to develop my skills in Bible study and personal devotions
❏ to belong to a small group that will support me in my growth
❏ to think through my values and priorities in light of God's will
❏ to wrestle with the next step in my spiritual journey with others who care

What are you willing to commit to in the way of disciplines during the time you are in this course?

❏ to complete the Bible study home assignment before the group meets
❏ to attend the group meetings except in cases of emergency
❏ to share in leading the group—taking my turn in rotation
❏ to keep confidential anything that is shared in the group
❏ to reach out to others who are not in a group and invite them to join us
❏ to participate in the group's mission of "giving birth" to a new group (see center section)

GROUP AGENDA

Every group meeting has three parts: (1) To Begin (10–15 minutes) to break the ice; (2) To Go Deeper (30 minutes) for Bible Study; and (3) To Close (15–30 minutes) for caring and prayer. When you get to the second part, have someone read the Scripture out loud and then divide into groups of 4 (4 at the dining table, 4 at the kitchen table, etc.). Then have everyone come back together for the third part.

TO BEGIN / 10–15 Min. (Choose 1 or 2)

1. Who is the letter writer in your family? How are you at writing letters?

2. What letter have you kept the longest?

3. If you had to talk tough to someone you loved who lived a long way from you, would you write them a letter or call them on the phone? What would be your first words?

TO GO DEEPER / 30 Min. (Choose 2 or 3)

1. Let each person choose one of the READ or SEARCH questions from the "homework" to answer. (It's okay if more than one person chooses the same question.)

2. From what you learned in the book of Acts—and from the COMMENTS on the next page—how would you describe Paul's relationship to the church in Ephesus? If you were a member of that church, how do you think you would feel about receiving this letter?

3. Who is one person who helped you get started in the Christian life? How did he or she encourage you?

4. On a scale of 1 (low) to 10 (high), how "faithful" (see v. 1) have you been to Jesus Christ lately?

TO CLOSE / 15–30 Min.

1. What did you check under APPLY for the goals you would like to work on during this course?

2. What disciplines are you willing to commit to (second question in APPLY)?

3. Where do you need a little "grace and peace" in your life right now?

4. How can the group pray for you?

NOTES

Summary. Paul begins this epistle in the way most Greek letters began—by naming the sender and the recipients, and then by offering a brief greeting. He does alter the standard greeting somewhat, however, in order to make it distinctly Christian.

1:1 *Paul.* From the earliest centuries, the tradition of the church has been that Paul was the author of this letter which bears his name. However, in recent years some scholars have suggested that a disciple of Paul's actually wrote Ephesians. (See the discussion of Style in the Introduction.) But as F.F. Bruce put it: "The man who could write Ephesians must have been the apostle's equal, if not his superior, in mental stature and spiritual insight ... of such a second Paul early Christian history has no knowledge."

apostle. Apostles are much like ambassadors. They are chosen by the king (in this case Jesus) to represent him and are given power to act in his name. This was the title that was given the original Twelve (Luke 6:13) and then later to Paul (Gal. 1:11–24). By using this title, Paul indicates that he is writing with the authority of Jesus Christ.

Christ Jesus. Markus Barth translates this phrase, "the Messiah Jesus." He does so because the Greek word *christos* (which can be translated as either "Christ" or "Messiah") comes *before* the name, and thus is used as a title and not as part of Jesus' proper name. Paul here emphasizes Jesus' messianic nature because "Ephesians more than any other New Testament epistle, will press the point that Gentiles receive no salvation other than the one they share with Israel and receive through the Messiah. It is the salvation first promised and given to this people alone: Israel." (Barth). See also Matthew 16:16 and Acts 2:36.

by the will of God. A person did not get to be an apostle by volunteering for the job. Instead, it is Jesus who both calls and commissions a person to be an apostle. The epistle to the Ephesians contains more references to the will of God than any other book in the New Testament with the exception of the much longer Gospel of John (see Eph. 1:5,9,11; 5:17; 6:6).

the saints. This term (which can also be translated as "the holy") was originally used as a title for the people of Israel who were understood to be those whom God set apart ("made holy") for his own service. But here Paul bestows it on Gentile Christians as well, since they have been sanctified ("made holy") through Jesus the Messiah. This word is sometimes understood to refer just to those people who seem especially pious, people who might be considered "elite Christians." In fact, it refers to *all* of God's people and conveys the sense that each one of them has been "set apart" (which is the root meaning of "holy") to be his special person.

in Ephesus. As was indicated in the introductory material, these words are not found in the oldest Greek manuscripts of this epistle nor in other early and reliable texts. Barth says, "Only if Gentile-born members of the Ephesian congregation who were converted and baptized after Paul had left the city for the last time are being addressed in this epistle can the authenticity of the words 'in Ephesus' be upheld."

the faithful. The Christians to whom this letter is sent are not only called "the saints" but they are also called "the faithful." The Greek adjective *pistos* which is used here "... can have either an active meaning ('trusting,' 'having faith') or a passive ('trustworthy,' 'being faithful'). The RSV chooses the passive here, but the active seems better since God's people are 'the household of faith' (Gal. 6:10), united by their common trust in God through Jesus Christ. At the same time, J. Armitage Robinson may be right in suggesting that 'the two senses of *pistis*, "Belief" and "fidelity," appear to be blended.' Certainly, it is hard to imagine a believer who is not himself believable, or a trustworthy Christian who has not learned trustworthiness from him in whom he has put his trust" (Stott).

1:2 *Grace and peace.* At this point in a letter, typically the writer said "rejoice" (and used the Greek word *chairein*). Paul uses a slightly different word from the same root (*charis*), which means "grace." Then to this modified Greek opening he adds the typical Hebrew greeting *Shalom,* or "peace." In this way he Christianized the introduction of his letter. "Grace" refers to the undeserved favor of God freely given as a gift. "Peace" refers to the reconciliation of sinners to God and others. Taken together they define the central theme of Ephesians: peace through grace.

Lord. This is the second title given to Jesus. Not only is he the Messiah, but he is the Lord. The title "Lord" was used in many ways in the first century. It was the equivalent of "Sir" or "Mr." (see Matt. 25:11). It was the title given to a landowner (see Matt. 20:8). It was used for kings and rulers (see Acts 25:26). But it is also the same word that is used in the Greek translation of the Old Testament for the name of God.

COMMENTS
The City and Church of Ephesus
The city of Ephesus was the capital of the Roman province of Asia. It was a large, bustling, secular city situated on the west coast of Asia Minor (modern Turkey) on the Aegean Sea. Originally a Greek colony, by Roman times it had become a center for international trade, largely as a result of its fine, natural harbor.

Its key architectural feature was the Temple of Artemis (or Diana), which was considered one of the seven wonders of the ancient world. The image of Artemis was thought to have descended from heaven (Acts 19:35). There was also a huge, outdoor Greek theatre, the largest in the world, capable of holding 50,000 people—as well as a stadium where fights, races and other athletic contests were held.

Paul's first visit to Ephesus was brief—little more than a reconnaissance trip (Acts 18:18–22). He later returned during his third missionary journey (see map on page 11) and spent over two years there. His ministry was effective and controversial. After three months in the synagogue, he was forced out and so took up residence in the lecture hall of Tyrannus (Acts 19:8–9). Paul probably worked as a tentmaker in the mornings and lecturer in the afternoons. News of his message spread throughout Asia Minor (Acts 19:10). Extraordinary and miraculous things happened. Handkerchiefs touched by him were used to cure the sick (Acts 19:11–12). Demons were cast out by the name of Jesus, even by Jewish exorcists (Acts 19:13–17). Pagan converts burned their books of magic (Acts 19:18–20).

Eventually a riot broke out in Ephesus over Paul. Demetrius, a silversmith, organized a citywide protest. He charged that Paul's success posed a threat to the economic well-being of craftsmen who made their living from the worshipers of Artemis (Acts 19:23–41). As a result, Paul moved on to Macedonia. But by this time the church was firmly established.

Paul never visited Ephesus again. He did, however, stop at the nearby port of Miletus on his return to Jerusalem. He called the Ephesian elders to him there and gave a moving farewell address (Acts 20:13–38). Later on, Paul would write 1 and 2 Timothy in an attempt to deal with false teaching that had arisen in Ephesus—as he had warned in his farewell address might happen (Acts 20:28–31). His words and Timothy's ministry were apparently successful. The book of Revelation records that the Ephesians resisted false teaching—though they had lost their first love (Rev. 2:1–7).

UNIT 2—Spiritual Blessings in Christ / Eph. 1:3-14

Spiritual Blessings in Christ

³*Praise be to the God and Father of our Lord Jesus Christ, who has blessed us in the heavenly realms with every spiritual blessing in Christ. ⁴For he chose us in him before the creation of the world to be holy and blameless in his sight. In love ⁵heª predestined us to be adopted as his sons through Jesus Christ, in accordance with his pleasure and will—⁶to the praise of his glorious grace, which he has freely given us in the One he loves. ⁷In him we have redemption through his blood, the forgiveness of sins, in accordance with the riches of God's grace ⁸that he lavished on us with all wisdom and understanding. ⁹And heᵇ made known to us the mystery of his will according to his good pleasure, which he purposed in Christ, ¹⁰to be put into effect when the times will have reached their fulfillment—to bring all things in heaven and on earth together under one head, even Christ.*

¹¹*In him we were also chosen,ᶜ having been predestined according to the plan of him who works out everything in conformity with the purpose of his will, ¹²in order that we, who were the first to hope in Christ, might be for the praise of his glory. ¹³And you also were included in Christ when you heard the word of truth, the gospel of your salvation. Having believed, you were marked in him with a seal, the promised Holy Spirit, ¹⁴who is a deposit guaranteeing our inheritance until the redemption of those who are God's possession—to the praise of his glory.*

ª4,5 Or *sight in love.* ⁵He   ᵇ8,9 Or *us. With all wisdom and understanding,* ⁹*he*   ᶜ11 Or *were made heirs*

READ

First Reading / First Impressions: Since this was originally one long sentence (see "Summary" on page 18), Paul reminds me here of a(n):

❏ sports announcer extolling a favorite star

❏ essay for which I got a "D" for run-on sentences

❏ pastor reciting a ritualized prayer

❏ teenager talking about his new love

Second Reading / Big Idea: In this paragraph-long sentence, what seems to be a key verse? Why?

SEARCH

1. In your own words, describe the "blessings of Christ" described in this passage.

2. Based on this passage, fill in this chart with the PAST, PRESENT and FUTURE activities which FATHER, SON and HOLY SPIRIT do for our salvation.

	Father	Son	Holy Spirit
Past			
Present			
Future			

3. How do you resolve the fact that God chose you "before the creation of the world" with your own free will to receive or not receive his grace (see notes on v. 4 and v. 5)?

4. In all that God is doing for us, what is his motivation (vv. 4,12)? His purpose (vv. 9–10)?

motivation	purpose

5. From the human point of view, what is the key to inheriting all God has done for us (vv. 12–13)?

APPLY

Try to express in one sentence, "My purpose in life as a Christian is to ..."

One specific way I could reflect that purpose this week is:

GROUP AGENDA

Every group meeting has three parts: (1) To Begin (10–15 minutes) to break the ice; (2) To Go Deeper (30 minutes) for Bible Study; and (3) To Close (15–30 minutes) for caring and prayer. When you get to the second part, have someone read the Scripture out loud and then divide into groups of 4 (4 at the dining table, 4 at the kitchen table, etc.). Then have everyone come back together for the third part.

TO BEGIN / 10–15 Min. (Choose 1 or 2)

1. What is the best medicine for you when you get down in the dumps?

2. What is your favorite movie or TV show—the one that really lifts your spirits?

3. Who deserves an Academy Award in your family for always looking on the bright side of things?

TO GO DEEPER / 30 Min. (Choose 2 or 3)

1. If you have completed the SEARCH section, what stands out the most to you from these questions?

2. What did you find out from the reference notes about God "choosing" people? How does it make you feel to hear that God chose you "before the creation of the world to be holy and blameless in his sight"?

3. When did you come to appreciate all that God has done for you in Jesus Christ?

4. What is the most exciting or positive thing about your relationship with God right now?

5. CASE STUDY: Jenny, adopted as a baby, is now in high school. In light of being adopted, she is struggling with her identity and worth. How could you use this passage to help Jenny?

TO CLOSE / 15–30 Min.

1. Who could you invite to this group next week?

2. Share your answers to the two questions in APPLY.

3. How can the group pray for you this week?

NOTES

Summary. In most of Paul's letters, the salutation is followed by a word of thanksgiving. On occasion, Paul added to this thanksgiving a blessing. But here he departs from his usual format. He begins with a long blessing (1:3–14) and follows with an equally long thanksgiving (1:15–23). The blessing (which will be studied in this unit) is, in Greek, a single, complex sentence which seems to tumble out of Paul's lips. This is the first of several "monster sentences" (as Markus Barth calls them). So intent is Paul on praising the work of God in the lives of Christians he simply heaps phrase upon phrase, so his words defy careful grammatical or conceptual analysis. In verses 3–6 his focus is on the past election by God the Father. In verses 7–12 he shifts to the present redemptive activity by Jesus Christ the Son, while in verses 13–14 his concern is with the future inheritance guaranteed by the Holy Spirit.

1:3 *Praise.* This paragraph is a hymn of praise to God. This is what a blessing is—a shout of praise to God for what he has done on behalf of his people. Paul "blesses" God for his work of grace. The verb "praise" can also be translated "to speak well of" and carries the idea of thanking, glorifying and singing praises of the one who is the object of this gratitude.

God. God is the subject of virtually every main verb in this passage. At those places where the verbs are passive (e.g. vv. 11 and 13), it is the work of God that is being described. It is God's work of love, grace and redemption that generates all this praise.

Jesus Christ. It is in and through Jesus that God's work of love, grace and redemption is performed. In the first 14 verses Jesus is named or referred to some 15 times. Eleven times the phrase "in Christ" or "in him" is used.

has blessed us. The tense of the Greek verb indicates that what is in view here is a single, past action on God's part. "Every blessing of the Holy Spirit has been given us by the Father if we are in the Son. No blessing has been withheld from us. Of course we still have to grow into maturity in Christ, and be transformed into his image, and explore the riches of our inheritance in him. Of course, too, God may grant us many deeper and richer experiences of himself on the way. Nevertheless already, if we are in Christ, every spiritual blessing is ours" (Stott).

the heavenly realms. This is a phrase used by Paul only in Ephesians, where it occurs five times (1:3,20; 2:6; 3:10; 6:12). It refers to the unseen world of spiritual reality.

spiritual blessing. This phrase may mean that the blessing God gave was *spiritual,* in contrast to the Old Testament stress on *material* blessing. However, the phrase "spiritual blessing" could also mean "every blessing of the *Holy Spirit.*" In this case, in these first verses the work of the whole Trinity is seen—God the Father, God the Son, and God the Holy Spirit.

1:4 *he chose us in him.* "God put us and Christ together in his mind. He determined to make us (who did not yet exist) his own children through the redeeming work of Christ (which had not yet taken place)" (Stott).

holy and blameless. In Ephesians 5:27 and Colossians 1:22 this phrase is used to define the goal of the Christian life: people who have been made perfect and whole. (The Greek word translated here as "blameless" is used to describe the kind of animal that was acceptable as an offering to God— one that was perfect and without blemish.) In other words, men and women are chosen by God to be and to become a certain kind of person.

1:5 *predestined.* Literally "marked out beforehand." Predestination is a difficult but thoroughly biblical doctrine, characteristic of God's activity in the Old Testament in choosing Israel (Ex. 19:4–6; Deut. 7:6–11; Isa. 42:1; 43:1) and in the New Testament in choosing the church, which is the new Israel.

adopted. This was a common Roman (but not Jewish) custom in which a child was given all the rights of the adoptive family by grace, not by merit (or birth).

his sons. The purpose of predestination is that people become the sons and daughters (the term "sons" is, of course, generic and intended to include both men and women) of God. This is what they are chosen to be—children of God. In turn, such children are destined to become holy and blameless.

his pleasure and will. This phrase carries with it the sense that God goes about such choosing with great joy. This is not the arbitrary action of an impersonal potentate.

1:6 *to the praise of his glorious grace.* "Not only the root and means of God's decision and work are located in God himself but also their purpose. ... This does not mean that God wants ultimately to praise himself. Self-laudation is according to Paul (Rom. 2:17–29) a caricature of the word and essence of 'praising.' God wants to be praised by the children he

has adopted. It is their bliss which he seeks. So long and intensively does he shower grace on them that finally they cannot help but sing paeans to his splendid grace. His joy and pleasure in doing good is only fulfilled when they show themselves utterly pleased. Therefore he does not act like a tyrant who suppresses the freedom of his subjects and yet likes nothing better than sycophants praising his generous gifts. The praise God's people are to give is the enthusiastic applause and cheers of captives who have been given freedom (1:7,14; 3:12)" (Barth).

1:7 *redemption.* The setting free (originally of prisoners or slaves) by payment of a ransom (in this case, Jesus' death in place of the sinner).

forgiveness of sins. The child of God is not only given freedom from the penalty of sin, but the sin itself is forgotten. Redemption and forgiveness go together.

1:9 *mystery.* Contrary to the normal use of the word, with its emphasis on a secret being kept, here the word focuses on the disclosure of what was once hidden but is now revealed by God. In this case the astonishing fact is that the final goal of history is for this hopelessly divided world (Jews against Gentiles, male against female, etc.) to be united under Christ.

1:10 *to bring ... together.* From a Greek word meaning "to sum up" as in the conclusion of a speech or a column of figures; a gathering together of the pieces into a whole.

1:11–13 *we ... you.* Jewish Christians who first believed (*we*) are now joined by Gentile believers (*you*), a clear sign traditional barriers are crumbling.

1:13 *seal.* A mark placed by an owner on a package, a cow, or even a slave. The cults in the first century sometimes tattooed a mark on their devotees. For the Jews, circumcision was such a seal (Rom. 4:11); for Christians the Holy Spirit is his or her seal.

promised Holy Spirit. The Spirit is not only "promised," but the "seal" whereby the Christian is marked out as belonging to God and the "guarantee" of that Christian's future inheritance. The Holy Spirit was promised in the Old Testament (see Ezek. 36:27; Joel 2:28) and by Jesus (see Luke 24:49; John 14–16; Acts 1:4–5; 2:33,38–39; Gal. 3:14).

1:14 *deposit.* A down payment (here the experience of the Holy Spirit) which guarantees ultimate ownership by God.

UNIT 3—Thanksgiving & Prayer / Eph. 1:15-23

Thanksgiving and Prayer

¹⁵For this reason, ever since I heard about your faith in the Lord Jesus and your love for all the saints, ¹⁶I have not stopped giving thanks for you, remembering you in my prayers. ¹⁷I keep asking that the God of our Lord Jesus Christ, the glorious Father, may give you the Spiritᵃ of wisdom and revelation, so that you may know him better. ¹⁸I pray also that the eyes of your heart may be enlightened in order that you may know the hope to which he has called you, the riches of his glorious inheritance in the saints, ¹⁹and his incomparably great power for us who believe. That power is like the working of his mighty strength, ²⁰which he exerted in Christ when he raised him from the dead and seated him at his right hand in the heavenly realms, ²¹far above all rule and authority, power and dominion, and every title that can be given, not only in the present age but also in the one to come. ²²And God placed all things under his feet and appointed him to be head over everything for the church, ²³which is his body, the fullness of him who fills everything in every way.

ᵃ17 Or *a spirit*

READ

First Reading / First Impressions: What are your impressions of Paul's prayer here?

❏ It's so cosmic, I'm not sure what he's asking for. ❏ It's a lot broader than mine are!

❏ Oh, we pray like this all the time in my church. ❏ It's more praise than prayer.

Second Reading / Big Idea: What are two or three words that capture what Paul is praying for these people?

SEARCH

1. What are the two characteristics that mark this church (v. 15)?

2. How would you express Paul's prayer (vv. 17–19) in your own words?

3. What qualities would you expect to see in people for whom prayers like this were answered?

4. From verses 19b–23, what facts do you learn about Jesus (see notes)?

5. Given that Christians were a "minority party," why might these facts about Jesus which illustrate what Paul means by spiritual power (v. 19) be especially important?

6. What are some implications that come to mind from the fact that the church is Christ's "body" on earth (vv. 22–23)?

APPLY

In this upcoming week, what are two or three ways you will express your "faith in Jesus" and "love for all the saints"?

In what ways would you like to see the prayer of verses 17–19 fulfilled in your life?

For example, "I need wisdom for …"

"I need hope for …"

"I need power for …"

GROUP AGENDA

NOTES

Every group meeting has three parts: (1) To Begin (10–15 minutes) to break the ice; (2) To Go Deeper (30 minutes) for Bible Study; and (3) To Close (15–30 minutes) for caring and prayer. When you get to the second part, have someone read the Scripture out loud and then divide into groups of 4 (4 at the dining table, 4 at the kitchen table, etc.). Then have everyone come back together for the third part.

TO BEGIN / 10–15 Min. (Choose 1 or 2)
1. What do you remember the most about Thanksgiving Day when you were a child?

2. If you wear glasses, how did you (or your parents) first realize your eyesight needed help?

3. Who believed in you, even when you didn't believe in yourself?

TO GO DEEPER / 30 Min. (Choose 2 or 3)
1. If you have completed the "homework," choose one of the READ or SEARCH questions and share your answer. (It's okay if more than one person chooses the same question.)

2. How does this prayer tie into the previous passage where Paul describes all of the things that are true of the Christian (see "Summary" in notes)?

3. How do you feel about the amazing truths about Jesus Christ found in this passage?

4. In prayer, do you tend to concentrate on praise or problems?

5. CASE STUDY: Your friend puts himself down all the time as "no good, worthless—a nobody." Even when it comes to spiritual things, he talks about how "bad" and "worthless" he is. What is it going to take to turn this person around?

TO CLOSE / 15–30 Min.
1. Has your group started on the six steps to fulfilling your mission—from the center section?

2. Share your answer to one of the questions in APPLY.

3. In light of the power available to Christians (v. 19), what is your favorite excuse for "operating on one or two cylinders"?

4. How would you like the group to pray for you?

Summary. Having praised the triune God for the incredible activity in, through and on behalf of his people (vv. 3–14), Paul now prays that the Christians to whom he writes will grasp the magnitude of what has been done for them. "Enlightenment" is what he wants for them. He craves for them that they be able to "see" what is so (vv. 17–18). He wants them to grasp the hope to which they have been called; the glory of their inheritance; and the magnitude of God's power. He ends this section focusing in particular on this last point, God's power. He struggles to express how overwhelming and how comprehensive this power is. This is the second of Paul's "monster sentences." It runs from verse 15 straight through to verse 23. The NIV has broken it up into five English sentences in order to help people grasp what is being said.

1:15 *For this reason.* The prayer which follows springs directly from the vision in verses 3–14 of the spiritual blessings given to us.

ever since I heard about. Paul does not know the people to whom he writes. As discussed in the Introduction, they may be Christians in Asia Minor converted as the power of his ministry radiated outward from Ephesus (Acts 19:10); or they may be new Gentile Christians in Ephesus converted after Paul left that region.

your faith ... and your love. The best Greek manuscripts omit the phrase "your love" in which case this verse would be translated as Markus Barth does: "after hearing of the faithfulness (shown) among you to the Lord Jesus and toward all the saints ... ." If this is the correct rendering then the cause of Paul's thankfulness is their two-fold faithfulness. They are faithful to Christ and they are faithful to one another. If Paul did include the phrase "your love" (its absence in the early manuscripts can easily be explained as a not untypical form of scribal error), then we have the familiar idea that a Christian is one who has faith in Christ and who loves other people. This later version parallels exactly Colossians 1:4.

1:16 *thanks.* Paul's response to these new Christians is one of profound thankfulness ("I have not stopped giving thanks") because in them the same wonderful activity of God described in verses 3–14 has happened, is happening and will happen. It is his thankfulness for this miracle of grace that compels him immediately to ask for enlightenment for them. He wants them to grasp the wonder of what has happened.

1:17 wisdom and revelation. Awareness of all these spiritual blessings will not necessarily come via logical dedication, nor solely as a result of experience. There must also be an inner work of God by which individuals are enabled to "see" what is going on.

so that you may know him better. Paul asks for two types of illumination. This is the first. He prays not that they will know about God, but that they will know him better. They have already entered into a relationship with God. He wants that to deepen. Paul uses a composite Greek noun here which denotes "real, deep, and full knowledge as distinct from first awareness or superficial acquaintance" (Barth).

1:18 I pray also. This is his second prayer for insight. Now he wants them to grasp three things in particular that flow out of this personal relationship with God.

the eyes of your heart. The heart was understood to be not simply an organ that pumped blood. It was the very center of one's personality. Paul wants this illumination to strike right to the core of a person's being.

enlightened. The Greek tense of this verb signifies "not only an action by God, but a status already created by that action" (Barth).

the hope to which he has called you. This is the first of the three gifts which result from knowing God. The emphasis is not so much on "hoping" (the subjective feeling of optimism for the future) as it is on the external reality that urges the Christian forward into the future. The mention of calling refers back to 1:4–5 and the idea of having been chosen to be holy and without blame, predestined to be adopted as God's sons and daughters. These phrases seem to define well the objective substance of this hope; i.e. they are God's children and they will be holy and not held accountable for their sins.

the riches of his glorious inheritance in the saints. This is the second benefit derived from knowing God. The inheritance in mind here might refer to Christians as God's own inheritance or possession as they are often spoken of in the Old Testament (see Deut. 32:9). More likely the idea is parallel to that in Colossians 1:12, and the reference is to the riches beyond imagination which God has reserved for his people (see also 1 Peter 1:4).

1:19 his incomparably great power. This is the third gift. "If God's 'call' looks back to the beginning, and God's 'inheritance' looks on to the end, then surely God's 'power' spans the interim period in between. It is on this that the apostle concentrates, for only God's power can fulfill the expectation which belongs to his call and brings us safely to the riches of the glory of the final inheritance he will give us in heaven" (Stott).

That power is like. At this point in his prayer, language fails Paul. How can he possibly describe the greatness of God's power? It is so beyond anything that is known. His answer is two-fold. First, he simply lumps together in an almost untranslatable phrase four Greek synonyms for power. Verse 19b reads literally, "the power is like the energy of the might of his strength." The first word is *dunamis* (from which "dynamite" is derived) or "power" and it denotes the ability to accomplish what is begun. The second word is *energeia* (from which "energy" is derived) or "working" and it means brute strength or muscle. The third word is *kratos* or "strength" and refers to the ability to face obstacles and overcome them. The final word is *ischus* or "mighty" and refers to the actual use of power. Second, having said "God's power is like every conception you have ever had of power," Paul then points to three acts in history when that power was displayed. It was seen in the past in God's act of raising Christ from the dead. It is seen now in the present enthronement of Christ as King. It is also seen in the way Christ is head over the church.

1:20 raised him from the dead. Jesus was really dead, buried in a tomb. But so mighty is God's power that it burst the bonds of death. Even centuries later one can look back at that empty tomb (for which no adequate explanation apart from resurrection has ever been offered) and begin to grasp the extent and nature of God's power.

seated him at his right hand. Jesus is now the King who reigns in absolute power. One day that reign will result in the bringing together of all things under him (1:10). See Psalm 110:1 and Hebrews 2:5–9.

1:21 rule and authority, power and dominion, and every title that can be given. Paul wants to be quite clear that there is no power by any name—be it angelic or demonic, natural or supernatural, from the past or in the future—that stands outside the scope of Christ's powerful reign.

1:22 head over everything for the church. The third act of power is seen in the appointing of Jesus, who is over all things, as head of the church—which is, in fact, his very body.

UNIT 4—Made Alive in Christ / Ephesians 2:1-10

Made Alive in Christ

2 As for you, you were dead in your transgressions and sins, ²in which you used to live when you followed the ways of this world and of the ruler of the kingdom of the air, the spirit who is now at work in those who are disobedient. ³All of us also lived among them at one time, gratifying the cravings of our sinful nature° and following its desires and thoughts. Like the rest, we were by nature objects of wrath. ⁴But because of his great love for us, God, who is rich in mercy, ⁵made us alive with Christ even when we were dead in transgressions—it is by grace you have been saved. ⁶And God raised us up with Christ and seated us with him in the heavenly realms in Christ Jesus, ⁷in order that in the coming ages he might show the incomparable riches of his grace, expressed in his kindness to us in Christ Jesus. ⁸For it is by grace you have been saved, through faith—and this not from yourselves, it is the gift of God—⁹not by works, so that no one can boast. ¹⁰For we are God's workmanship, created in Christ Jesus to do good works, which God prepared in advance for us to do.

°3 Or *our flesh*

READ

First Reading / First Impressions: If Paul was preaching this passage, what tone of voice would he use in:

> verses 1–3?

> verses 4–10?

Second Reading / Big Idea: What do you think is the key word in:

> verses 1–3?

> verses 4–10?

SEARCH

1. What does Paul mean by describing people without Christ as "dead" (v. 1; see note)?

2. What does he mean by the influences he says dominate the lives of people without Christ (v. 2)?

> The world

> The ruler of the kingdom of the air

3. What are the parallels between what God did for Jesus (1:20–22) and what he does for us?

(v. 5)

(v. 6)

4. From the way "grace" is used in verses 5,7 and 8, how would you define what it means (see note on v. 5)?

5. What is Paul's point in verses 8–9, and how does this fit with verse 10 (see notes for vv. 8–9)?

6. How would you paraphrase God's purpose in this passage?

7. How might you use verse 10 to describe what your purpose in life is to be?

APPLY

How is your life different now than it was before you became a Christian?

What are some of the good works which God has created for you to fulfill in your ...
(Hint: Consider specific needs people have and what resources you have to meet those needs.)

family?

church?

local community?

world community?

GROUP AGENDA

After the first part, read the Scripture out loud and divide into groups of 4. Then come back together for the third part.

TO BEGIN / 10–15 Min. (Choose 1 or 2)

1. Who has the record for the most speeding tickets in your small group?

2. When you were a kid, did you ever get in hot water at school? What did your parents say?

3. Do you enjoy working with your hands? What have you made that you are most proud of?

TO GO DEEPER / 30 Min. (Choose 2 or 3)

1. If you've completed the homework, choose one of the READ or SEARCH questions to share. (It's okay if more than one person chooses the same question.)

2. What does faith have to do with being saved? How do good works fit in? How do the notes help you understand verses 8–10?

3. How would you divide this passage into three time periods: (a) past, (b) present and (c) future?

4. How would you describe each of these periods in your own life and experience?

5. How does the fact that God views us with grace, mercy, love and kindness affect your desire to respond to him? Your self-image? Your ability to cope with hard times? Or do you feel more like you must be an "object of wrath" (v. 3)? Why?

6. CASE STUDY: Your friend, Doug, has it all. Money, a great job, and good looks. One day he says to you, "It's all meaningless. I don't know what life's all about." What's the message here for him?

TO CLOSE / 15–30 Min.

1. Has your group taken the survey for small groups in your church (see page M15 in the center section)? If so, what are you going to do as a result?

2. Share your answer to one of the questions in APPLY.

3. How can the group pray for you?

NOTES

Summary. In 2:1–10, Paul is showing that the ultimate reconciliation of all things in Christ Jesus, described in chapter one (1:9–10,20–22), is guaranteed by the reconciliation that has already been effected between God and people. In 2:11–22, he will further demonstrate this fact by pointing to the (unprecedented) reconciliation between Jew and Gentile, which likewise confirms that ultimate reconciliation will, indeed, occur. In 2:1–10, Paul describes this reconciliation between God and people by means of a series of triple contrasts.

2:1–3 Here are his first two triple descriptions. Humanity faces a triple peril: we are dead because of sin (v. 1), we are enslaved to sin (vv. 2–3a), and we face condemnation (wrath) for our sin (v. 3b). In describing our slavery to sin, he points out that we were under the triple powers of the world, the devil, and the flesh.

2:1 *As for you.* The "you" refers to the Gentiles in Asia Minor to whom Paul was writing. This is made clear in verse 11 where he refers to "you who are Gentiles by birth." However, verses 1–3 is not just a portrait of decadent pagans. In verse 3a Paul says "all of us" lived the same way, thus including himself and his fellow Jews in this description. And in verse 3b he refers to "the rest," indicating that the whole human race is like this.

dead. They were spiritually dead, i.e., humanity in general is out of tune with God's ways and out of fellowship with God himself. Paul means this literally, not metaphorically. Without a relationship with God, people are dead within. Paul will go on to explain in verse 5 how men and women can be raised from the dead.

transgressions and sins. These two words give a comprehensive view of the human evil by touching on both its positive and negative aspects. "Transgressions" refers to active wrongdoing. The image behind this word is of a person crossing a boundary fence into a forbidden field, or of a person wandering off the true path into the wrong way. These are "sins of commission." The word "sins," on the other hand, refers to passive failure. The core image here is of an archer shooting arrows at a target, none of which hit the bullseye. They all "fall short." These are "sins of omission."

2:2 *followed.* Literally, "walked." Paul means that people followed a particular path. The word does not mean "aimless strolling around" but has the same sense of a deliberate choice of direction. The path one follows determines the way one lives in an ethical and moral sense. In contrast to "following the ways of this world," Jesus calls people to follow him and his teaching.

the ways of this world. Literally, "according to the age of this world." The idea of "this age" refers to the fact that there would be two ages—this present evil age and a future age in which God would reign. "This world" refers to the system of values and perspectives around which society is organized and which is hostile to God. "The ways of this world" is the first power to which people outside Christ are enslaved.

ruler of the kingdom of the air. This is the first of several references in Ephesians to Satan. He is called "the devil" in 4:27 and 6:11; and "the evil one" in 6:16. Here we learn that he is reigning monarch over a real kingdom, and that his kingdom is located in "the air" or "atmosphere" ("the heavenly realms" in 6:12). The devil is the second power to which people are enslaved.

those who are disobedient. This is the main attribute of those who are "dead in ... transgressions and sins." They disobey God. Paul has just shown that God is the Ultimate Ruler. Still, they fail to live in accord with God's "way" and are in active rebellion against him.

2:3 *our sinful nature.* The word here is literally "the flesh" and it refers to self-centered human nature which expresses itself in destructive activities of both body and mind. This is the third bondage under which humans struggle.

wrath. "In the Bible the 'wrath' of God ... does not represent the intemperate outburst of an uncontrolled character. It is rather the temperature of God's love, the manifestation of his will and power to resist, to overcome, to burn away all that contradicts his counsels of love" (Barth). Notice that the "wrath" of God in verse 3 is immediately contrasted in verse 4 with the "love" of God.

2:4 *But because of his great love for us.* Love is God's reason for rescuing fallen humanity. (This same theme is struck in the Old Testament. See, for example, Deuteronomy 7:6–9.) This is the first of four words by which Paul explains God's motivation for reaching out to us.

mercy. Not only love, but (secondly) mercy motivates God. The Greek word, *eleos,* is used in the Greek Old Testament (Septuagint) to translate the Hebrew word *hesed,* which in English is "loving-kindness" (KJV) or "steadfast love" (RSV). Love and mercy are not distant but closely related.

2:5 *made us alive.* This is the first of three verbs which Paul coins to describe exactly what happens to us when we are "in Christ." We were made alive together with Christ, raised up together with Christ (v. 6a); and seated together with Christ (v. 6b). In other words, we share in Christ's resurrection, ascension and enthronement.

by grace. This resurrection from the dead cannot be earned. It is simply given. Grace is God's unmerited favor or gift to us. The Greek word for grace (*charis*) is used to translate the Hebrew word *hen* "which denotes the favor shown by a superior to an inferior. It describes God's love and the steadfastness with which he keeps the covenant" (Barth). Grace is the third reason God reaches out to us.

you have been saved. The tense of this verb (past participle) signifies a past action which has been completed. To be "saved" is how Paul describes being rescued or delivered from the triple peril of death, slavery and wrath. ✳

2:7 *in order that in the coming ages he might show.* The change in life and status brought about in the Ephesians (and all who follow Christ) is another visible demonstration of the greatness of God's power. Paul says God displays "the incomparable riches of his grace" by this work in humanity.

kindness. Not only do love, mercy and grace describe God's character (and so explain his saving action on people's behalf), but Paul adds kindness as the fourth element in this list of attributes.

2:8 *For it is by grace you have been saved.* This is the second time Paul acclaims this amazing fact (see also v. 5).

through faith. Salvation does not come about *because* of faith. Salvation comes by grace, *through* faith. Faith is simply a person's grateful response by which he or she reaches out and accepts the gift of grace which has been offered.

2:8–9 *not from yourselves ... not by works.* Salvation is not a reward for what a person has done. It is not the result of being good or keeping the Law. Works stand in opposition to grace, which is the true origin of salvation.

2:10 *good works.* Although good works do not save a person, they do flow from that person as a *result* of salvation.

UNIT 5—One in Christ / Ephesians 2:11-22

One in Christ

¹¹*Therefore, remember that formerly you who are Gentiles by birth and called "uncircumcised" by those who call themselves "the circumcision" (that done in the body by the hands of men)*—¹²*remember that at that time you were separate from Christ, excluded from citizenship in Israel and foreigners to the covenants of the promise, without hope and without God in the world.* ¹³*But now in Christ Jesus you who once were far away have been brought near through the blood of Christ.*

¹⁴*For he himself is our peace, who has made the two one and has destroyed the barrier, the dividing wall of hostility,* ¹⁵*by abolishing in his flesh the law with its commandments and regulations. His purpose was to create in himself one new man out of the two, thus making peace,* ¹⁶*and in this one body to reconcile both of them to God through the cross, by which he put to death their hostility.* ¹⁷*He came and preached peace to you who were far away and peace to those who were near.* ¹⁸*For through him we both have access to the Father by one Spirit.*

¹⁹*Consequently, you are no longer foreigners and aliens, but fellow citizens with God's people and members of God's household,* ²⁰*built on the foundation of the apostles and prophets, with Christ Jesus himself as the chief cornerstone.* ²¹*In him the whole building is joined together and rises to become a holy temple in the Lord.* ²²*And in him you too are being built together to become a dwelling in which God lives by his Spirit.*

READ

First Reading / First Impressions: Do you see the apostle Paul more like a parent, a coach or a pastor to the Ephesians?

Second Reading / Big Idea: What verse seems to sum up the meaning of this whole passage? Why?

SEARCH

1. Who are the two types of people referred to here (v. 11)?

2. What are the five strikes against the Gentiles in verse 12 (see notes for v. 12)?

   1.

   2.

3.

4.

5.

3. How did Jesus change all this (v. 13)?

4. How did this affect the Gentiles' relationship to the Jews (vv. 14,17–18)?

5. What is the significance of each of the images Paul uses to describe the Gentiles' new relationship with God and the Jews (see corresponding notes)?

Fellow citizens (v. 19)

Members of God's household (v. 19)

The temple of the Lord (v. 21)

APPLY

What is the message of this passage for your church?

What is the relationship in your life (or group of people) where you need to knock down the wall that separates you?

GROUP AGENDA

After the first part, read the Scripture out loud and divide into groups of 4. Then come back together for the third part.

TO BEGIN / 10–15 Min. (Choose 1 or 2)

1. How racially diverse was the neighborhood and community you grew up in?

2. What did it take to be part of the "in" group at your high school? To be part of the "out" group?

3. Have you ever been in a situation where you felt like an alien?

TO GO DEEPER / 30 Min. (Choose 2 or 3)

1. What impressed you from the homework and the reference notes about the amazing changes Christ brought to the world?

2. What is the difference between Hitler's idea of a super race and Paul's idea of "one body"?

3. In chapter one, Christ is referred to as the "head" of the body. What is he referred to in this passage? What is the significance of each?

4. If you could write an editorial for your local newspaper based on the truth you find in this passage, what would you want to say to your own community?

5. CASE STUDY: The Ku Klux Klan held a rally in your town. One of your coworkers went and was intrigued that the speaker kept saying they were Christians and used the Bible to support his white supremacist position. What might you share with him from this passage?

TO CLOSE / 15–30 Min.

1. Are you working on your mission as a group? Are you inviting new people to join you?

2. Share one or both of your answers in the APPLY section.

3. How can the group support you in prayer?

NOTES

Summary. Paul moves from the problem of human alienation from God (2:1–10) to the related problem of alienation between people themselves (2:11–22). In both cases, the problem is hostility (or enmity). In both cases, Christ is the one who, through his death, brings peace—first between God and people, but then, also, between human enemies. The particular focus of this section is on the deep hostility between Jew and Gentile. Paul begins by reminding the Gentiles of their five-fold alienation from God's plan for the world (vv. 11–12). But he then goes on to describe how Jesus' death overcame all that (vv. 13–18). Jesus abolished the Law which divided people from God and each other; he created a new humanity and he reconciled this new "race" to God. Paul concludes by describing, through three metaphors (kingdom, family, temple), the new reality which has emerged (vv. 19–22).

2:11 *remember that formerly.* The focus in verses 11–12 is on what the Gentiles once were, prior to the beginning of their spiritual quest.

"uncircumcised." This is a derogatory slur by which Gentiles were mocked. With this contemptuous nickname Jews were saying that the Gentiles' lack of "God's mark" on their bodies put them absolutely outside of God's kingdom, so they were to be despised.

"the circumcision." This is how Jews thought of themselves and was a term used with pride. Circumcision was the sign given to Abraham by which the covenant people were to be marked. This made the Jew different and special.

2:12 *separate from Christ.* The Gentiles had no hope of a coming Messiah who would make all things right. Instead, they considered themselves to be caught up in the deadly cycle of history which led nowhere. This separation from the hope of a Messiah was the first liability faced by Gentiles.

excluded from citizenship. Gentiles were not part of God's kingdom. Israel was a nation founded by God, consisting of his people; and Gentiles were outside that reality. This was their second liability.

foreigners to the covenants. Not only did Gentiles have no part in God's kingdom, they also stood outside all the amazing agreements (covenants) God made with his people (see for example Ex. 6:6–8; Deut. 28:9–14). This is the third liability.

without hope. During this particular historical era,

the Roman world experienced a profound loss of hope. The first century was inundated with mystery cults, all promising salvation from this despair. Living in fear of demons, people felt themselves to be mere playthings of the capricious gods. This lack of hope in the face of fear was the fourth liability.

without God. This is not to say that Gentiles were atheists (even though the word used here is *atheos*). On the contrary, they worshiped scores of deities. The problem was that they had no effective knowledge of the one true God. This is the final liability.

2:13 But now ... through the blood of Christ. Paul pinpoints how God's intervention into this seemingly hopeless situation occurred. It is as a result of Jesus' death on the cross that union with Christ is possible (see 1:7).

2:14 our peace. Jesus brings peace; that is, he creates harmony between human beings and God. He also creates harmony between human beings. He draws together those who consider each other to be enemies. He does this by being the one who stands between the alienated parties, bridging the gap that separates them.

the dividing wall. Paul has in mind an actual wall which existed in the temple in Jerusalem. The temple itself was built on an elevated area. The inner sanctuary was surrounded by the Court of the Priests. Beyond this was the Court of Israel (for men only) and then the Court of the Women. All these courts were on the same level as the temple; and each had a different degree of exclusivity. Ringing all the courts and some 19 steps below was the Court of the Gentiles. Here Gentiles could gaze up at the temple. But they could not approach it. They were cut off by a stone wall ("the dividing wall") bearing signs that warned in Greek and Latin that trespassing foreigners would be killed. Paul himself knew well this prohibition. He had nearly been lynched by a mob of Jews who were told he had taken a Gentile into the temple.

hostility. The ancient world abounded in hostility. There was enmity between Jew and Gentile, Greek and barbarian, men and women, slave and free. Christ ends each form of hostility.

2:15–16 By means of three key verbs ("abolish," "create," and "reconcile") Paul describes the three accomplishments of Christ on the cross whereby he destroys "the dividing wall of hostility."

2:15 the law with its commandments and regulations. The primary reference is to the thousands of rules and regulations which were in existence at the time of Christ by which Jewish leaders sought to define the "Law of Moses" (the first five books of the Old Testament). The belief was that only by keeping all these rules could one be counted "good" and therefore have fellowship with God.

one new man. In the place of divided humanity, Jesus creates a whole new quality of being, a new humanity. This does not mean that Jews became Gentiles nor that Gentiles became Jews. Both became Christians, "the third race" (see also Gal. 3:28 and Col. 3:11).

2:16 reconcile. This word means "to bring together estranged parties." In verse 14 the emphasis is on reconciling Jew to Gentile. Here the reference is to bringing both Jew and Gentile together with God.

2:18 access. In Greek, one form of this word is used to describe an individual whose job it is to usher a person into the presence of the king. Indeed, not only did Jesus open the way back to God (by his death, humanity was reconciled to God), he continues to provide the means whereby an ongoing and continuing relationship is possible.

2:19 foreigners. Nonresident aliens who were disliked by the native population and often held in suspicion.

aliens. These are residents in a foreign land. They pay taxes but have no legal standing and few rights.

fellow citizens. Whereas once the Gentiles were "excluded from citizenship in Israel" (v. 12), now they are members of God's kingdom. They now "belong."

members of God's household. In fact, they do not merely have a new legal status ("citizens"); their relationship is far more intimate. They've become family.

2:20 cornerstone. That stone which rested firmly on the foundation and tied two walls together, giving each its correct alignment. The temple in Jerusalem had massive cornerstones (one was nearly 40 feet long). The image might be of Jesus holding together Jew and Gentile, Old Testament and New Testament.

2:21 temple. The new temple is not like the old one, carved out of dead stone, beautiful but forbidding and exclusive. Rather, it is alive all over the world, inclusive of all, made up of the individuals in whom God dwells.

UNIT 6—Paul, Preacher to the Gentiles / Eph. 3:1-13

Paul the Preacher to the Gentiles

3 For this reason I, Paul, the prisoner of Christ Jesus for the sake of you Gentiles— ²Surely you have heard about the administration of God's grace that was given to me for you, ³that is, the mystery made known to me by revelation, as I have already written briefly. ⁴In reading this, then, you will be able to understand my insight into the mystery of Christ, ⁵which was not made known to men in other generations as it has now been revealed by the Spirit to God's holy apostles and prophets. ⁶This mystery is that through the gospel the Gentiles are heirs together with Israel, members together of one body, and sharers together in the promise in Christ Jesus.

⁷I became a servant of this gospel by the gift of God's grace given me through the working of his power. ⁸Although I am less than the least of all God's people, this grace was given me: to preach to the Gentiles the unsearchable riches of Christ, ⁹and to make plain to everyone the administration of this mystery, which for ages past was kept hidden in God, who created all things. ¹⁰His intent was that now, through the church, the manifold wisdom of God should be made known to the rulers and authorities in the heavenly realms, ¹¹according to his eternal purpose which he accomplished in Christ Jesus our Lord. ¹²In him and through faith in him we may approach God with freedom and confidence. ¹³I ask you, therefore, not to be discouraged because of my sufferings for you, which are your glory.

READ

First Reading / First Impressions: What would a typical modern psychologist think about Paul, based on this passage?

Second Reading / Big Idea: It seems here that Paul is ...
- ❏ filling in some missing information about himself.
- ❏ expanding on what he already said in chapter 2.
- ❏ getting off on a tangent.
- ❏ bragging.

SEARCH

1. Why is Paul in prison when he writes this letter (see Acts 21:17–29 and notes on v. 1)?

2. "Mystery" appears in verses 3,4,6 and 9. What facts about this "mystery" can you learn here (also see notes)?

Leadership Training Supplement

YOU ARE
HERE

BIRTH	GROWTH	RELEASE

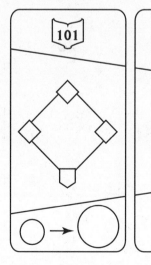

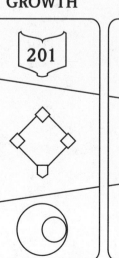

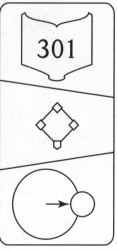

What is the game plan for your group in the 301 stage?

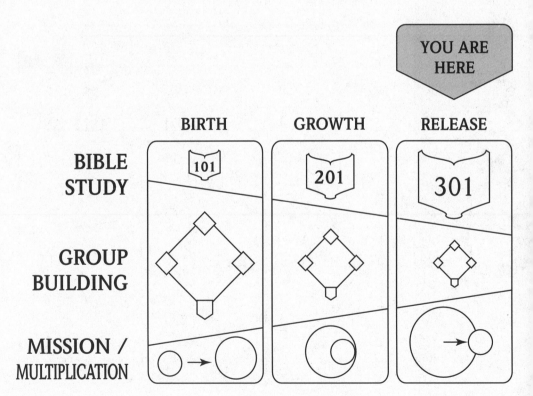

YOU ARE HERE

	BIRTH	GROWTH	RELEASE
BIBLE STUDY	101	201	301
GROUP BUILDING			
MISSION / MULTIPLICATION			

UNIT 5—One in Christ / Ephesians 2:11-22

One in Christ

"Therefore, remember that formerly you who are Gentiles by birth and called "uncircumcised" by those who call themselves "the circumcision" (that done in the body by the hands of men)—¹²remember that at that time you were separate from Christ, excluded from citizenship in Israel and foreigners to the covenants of the promise, without hope and without God in the world. ¹³But now in Christ Jesus you who once were far away have been brought near through the blood of Christ.

¹⁴For he himself is our peace, who has made the two one and has destroyed the barrier, the dividing wall of hostility, ¹⁵by abolishing in his flesh the law with its commandments and regulations. His purpose was to create in himself one new man out of the two, thus making peace, ¹⁶and in this one body to reconcile both of them to God through the cross, by which he put to death their hostility. ¹⁷He came and preached peace to you who were far away and peace to those who were near. ¹⁸For through him we both have access to the Father by one Spirit.

¹⁹Consequently, you are no longer foreigners and aliens, but fellow citizens with God's people and members of God's household, ²⁰built on the foundation of the apostles and prophets, with Christ Jesus himself as the chief cornerstone. ²¹In him the whole building is joined together and rises to become a holy temple in the Lord. ²²And in him you too are being built together to become a dwelling in which God lives by his Spirit.

READ

First Reading / First Impressions: Do you see the apostle Paul more like a parent, a coach or a pastor to the Ephesians?

Second Reading / Big Idea: What verse seems to sum up the meaning of this whole passage? Why?

(18) And pray with the Spirit ...

SEARCH

1. Who are the two types of people referred to here (v. 11)?

Those who take a stand

Those deceived by Satan's schemes.

2. What are the five strikes against the Gentiles in verse 12 (see notes for v. 12)?

1. *Separate from Christ*

2. *excluded from citizenship in Israel*

(3) C.1 Jesus is "Head of the Body" Significance?
C.2 = "Chief cornerstone"

v. (14) - in mind the actual "dividing wall" in Temple — a stone wall that kept
Gentiles out.

3. *foreigners to the covenants of promise*

4. *w/o hope*

5. *w/o God in the world.*

3. How did Jesus change all this (v. 13)?

Offered a new Covenant (blood)

4. How did this affect the Gentiles' relationship to the Jews (vv. 14,17–18)?

destroyed barrier & made them one.
He preached peace to them and gave them access to Father.

5. What is the significance of each of the images Paul uses to describe the Gentiles' new relationship with God and the Jews (see corresponding notes)?

Fellow citizens (v. 19) *once excluded, Gentiles are now included, belong, to Kingdom of God!*

Members of God's household (v. 19) *Not only citizens, but family (intimate)!*

The temple of the Lord (v. 21) *New temple is not dead stone that separates, but within people whom God dwells — alive all over the world!*

APPLY

What is the message of this passage for your church?

Christ is in the business of drawing those on the outside to Himself
. . . . & making them family.

What is the relationship in your life (or group of people) where you need to knock down the wall that separates you?

Are there any walls that separate people from us?

.

29

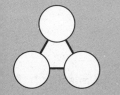

The 3-Legged Stool

The three essentials in a healthy small group are Bible Study, Group Building, and Mission / Multiplication. You need all three to stay balanced—like a 3-legged stool.
- To focus only on Bible Study will lead to scholasticism.
- To focus only on Group Building will lead to narcissism.
- To focus only on Mission will lead to burnout.

You need a game plan for the life cycle of the group where all of these elements are present in a purpose-driven strategy.

Bible Study

To develop the habit and skills for personal Bible Study.

TWO LEVELS: (1) Personal—on your own, and (2) Group study with your small group. In the personal Bible Study, you will be introduced to skills for reflection, self-inventory, creative writing and journaling.

Group Building

To move into discipleship with group accountability, shared leadership and depth community.

At the close of this course, the group building aspect will reach its goal with a "going-away" party. If there are other groups in the church in this program, the event would be for all groups. Otherwise, the group will have its own closing celebration and commissioning time.

Mission / Multiplication

To commission the members of the leadership team from your group who are going to start a new group.

This Leadership Training Supplement is about your mission project. In six steps, your group will be led through a decision-making process to discover the leadership team within your group to form a new group.

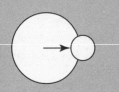

Mission / Multiplication

Where are you in the 3-stage life cycle of your mission?

You can't sit on a one-legged stool—or even a two-legged stool. It takes all three. A Bible Study and Care Group that doesn't have a MISSION will fall.

Birthing Cycle

The mission is to give birth to a new group at the conclusion of this course. In this 301 course, you are supposed to be at stage three. If you are not at stage three, you can still reach the mission goal if you stay focused.

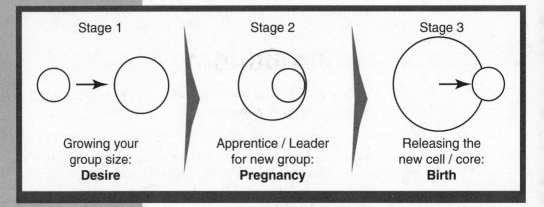

Stage 1	Stage 2	Stage 3
Growing your group size: **Desire**	Apprentice / Leader for new group: **Pregnancy**	Releasing the new cell / core: **Birth**

The birthing process begins with DESIRE. If you do not want to birth a new group, it will never happen. Desire keeps the group focused on inviting new people into your group every week—until your group grows to about 10 or 12 people.

The second stage is PREGNANCY. By recognizing the gifts of people in your group, you are able to designate two or three people who will ultimately be the missionaries in your group to form a new group. This is called the "leadership core."

The third stage is BIRTH—which takes place at the end of this course, when the whole group commissions the core or cell to move out and start the new group.

6 Steps to Birth a Group

Step 1

Desire

Is your group purpose-driven about mission?

Take this pop quiz and see how purpose-driven you are. Then, study the "four fallacies" about groups.

Step 2

Assessment

Is your church purpose-driven about groups?

Pinpoint where you are coming from and where most of the people in small groups in your church come from.

Step 3

Survey

Where's the itch for those in your church who are not involved in groups?

Take this churchwide survey to discover the felt needs of those in your church who do not seem to be interested in small groups.

Step 4

Brainstorming

What did you learn about your church from the survey?

Debrief the survey in the previous step to decide how your small group could make a difference in starting a new group.

Step 5

Barnstorming

Who are you going to invite?

Build a prospect list of people you think might be interested in joining a new group.

Step 6

Commissioning

Congratulations. You deserve a party.

Commission the leadership core from your group who are going to be your missionaries to start a new group. Then, for the rest of the "mother group," work on your covenant for starting over ... with a few empty chairs.

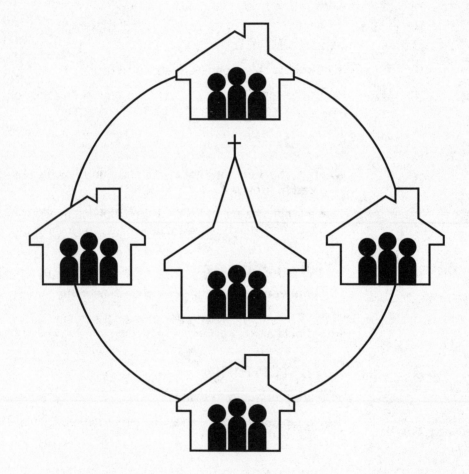

Step 1

Desire

Is your group purpose-driven about mission?

The greatest danger to any chain is its strongest link. This is especially true of Bible Study groups. The very depth of the study keeps new people from joining, or feeling comfortable when they join. In the end the group grows inward, becoming self-centered and spiritually insensitive.

To prevent this from happening in your group, take this pop quiz and share the results with your group.

	Yes	No
1. Are you a committed follower of Jesus Christ?	❏	❏
2. Do you believe that Jesus Christ wants you to share your faith with others?	❏	❏
3. Do you believe that every Christian needs to belong to a small, caring community where Jesus Christ is affirmed?	❏	❏
4. Do you know of people in your church who are not presently involved in a small group?	❏	❏
5. Do you know friends on the fringe of the church who need to belong to a life-sharing small group?	❏	❏
6. Do you believe that God has a will and plan for your life?	❏	❏
7. Are you willing to be open to what God might do through you in this small group?	❏	❏
8. Are you open to the possibility that God might use you to form a new group?	❏	❏

If you can't say "No" to any of these questions, consider yourself committed!

What Is a Small Group?

A Small Group is an intentional, face-to-face gathering of people in a similar stage of life at a regular time with a common purpose of discovering and growing in a relationship with Jesus Christ.

Small Groups are the disciple-making strategy of Flamingo Road Church. The behaviors of the 12 step strategy are the goals we want to achieve with each individual in small group. These goals are accomplished through a new members class (membership) and continues in a regular on-going small group (maturity, ministry and multiplication).

Keys to an Effective Small Group Ministry

1. Care for all people (members/guests) through organized active Care Groups.
2. Teach the Bible interactively while making life application.
3. Build a Servant Leadership Team.
4. Birth New Groups.

Commitments of all Small Group Leaders are ...

... all the behaviors represented in the 12 step strategy
... to lead their group to be an effective small group as mentioned above.
... use curriculum approved by small group pastor

Taken from the Small Group Training Manual of Flamingo Road Community Church, Fort Lauderdale, FL.

Four Fallacies About Small Groups

Are you suffering from one of these four misconceptions when it comes to small groups? Check yourself on these fallacies.

Fallacy #1: It takes 10 to 12 people to start a small group.

Wrong. The best size to start with is three or four people—which leaves room in the group for growth. Start "small" and pray that God will fill the "empty chair" ... and watch it happen.

Fallacy #2: It takes a lot of skill to lead a small group.

Wrong again. Sticking to the three-part tight agenda makes it possible for nearly anyone to lead a group. For certain support and recovery groups more skills are required, but the typical Bible Study and Care Group can be led by anyone with lots of heart and vision.

Fallacy #3: To assure confidentiality, the "door" should be closed after the first session.

For certain "high risk" groups this is true; but for the average Bible Study and Care Group all you need is the rule that "nothing that is said in the group is discussed outside of the group."

Fallacy #4: The longer the group lasts, the better it gets.

Not necessarily. The bell curve for effective small groups usually peaks in the second year. Unless new life is brought into the group, the group will decline in vitality. It is better to release the group (and become a reunion group) when it is at its peak than to run the risk of burnout.

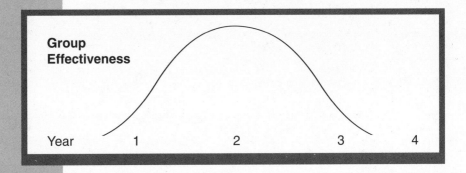

Group Effectiveness

Year   1   2   3   4

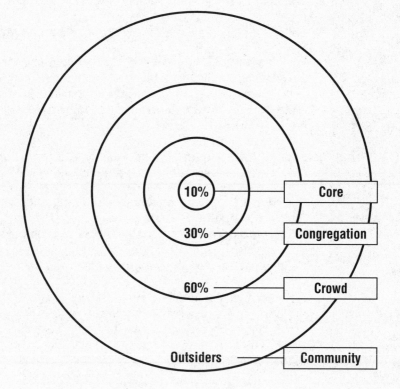

Step 2

Assessment

Is your church purpose-driven about groups?

Most of the people who come to small groups in the church are from the highly committed CORE of the church. How about your group?

Pinpoint Your Group

The graph on the opposite page represents the four types of people typically found in your church and in your community.

- **10% Core:** The "spiritual core" of the church and the church leadership.

- **30% Congregation:** Those who come to church regularly and are faithful in giving.

- **60% Crowd:** Those on the membership roles who attend only twice a year. They have fallen through the cracks.

- **Outside Community:** Those who live in the surrounding area but do not belong to any church.

Step 1: On the opposite page, put a series of dots in the appropriate circles where the members of your group come from.

Step 2: If you know of other small groups in your church, put some more dots on the graph to represent the people in those groups. When you are finished, stop and ask your group this question:

"Why do the groups in our church appeal only to the people who are represented by the dots on this graph?"

Four Kinds of Small Groups

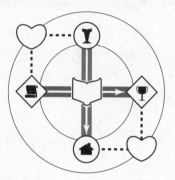

SUPPORT / RECOVERY GROUPS

- Felt needs
- Short-term
- Low-level commitment
- Seeker Bible Study

These groups are designed to appeal to hurting people on the fringe of the church and in the community.

PULPIT-BASED GROUPS

- Around the Scripture in the Sunday lesson
- With handout in Sunday bulletin
- With discussion questions
- No homework

These groups are designed to appeal to those who come to church and listen to the sermon but do not want to do homework.

DISCIPLESHIP / DEPTH BIBLE STUDY GROUPS

- Year-long commitment
- Depth Bible Study
- Homework required
- Curriculum based

These groups are designed to appeal to the 10% highly committed core of the church who are ready for discipleship.

COVENANT GROUPS

- Three-stage life cycle
- Renewal option
- Begins with 7-week contract
- Graded levels of Bible Study: 101, 201 and 301

Church Evaluation

You do NOT have to complete this assessment if you are not in the leadership core of your church, but it would be extremely valuable if your group does have members in the leadership core of your church.

1. Currently, what percentage of your church members are involved in small groups?

2. What kind of small groups are you offering in your church? (Study the four kinds of groups on the opposite page.)
   ❏ Support / Recovery Groups
   ❏ Pulpit-Based Groups
   ❏ Discipleship / Depth Bible Study Groups
   ❏ Three-stage Covenant Groups

3. Which statement below represents the position of your church on small groups?
   ❏ "Small Groups have never been on the drawing board at our church."
   ❏ "We have had small groups, but they fizzled."
   ❏ "Our church leadership has had negative experiences with small groups."
   ❏ "Small groups are the hope for our future."
   ❏ "We have Sunday school; that's plenty."

4. How would you describe the people who usually get involved in small groups?
   ❏ 10% Core   ❏ 30% Congregation   ❏ 60% Crowd

Risk and Supervision
This depends on the risk level of the group—the higher the risk, the higher the supervision. For the typical Bible Study group ⬜, pulpit-based group ⓨ, or covenant group ◈ (where there is little risk), supervision is minimal. For some support groups ♡ and all recovery groups ⚡, training and supervision are required.

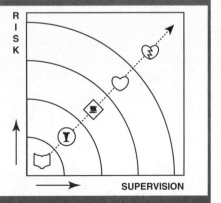

Step 3

Survey

Where's the itch for those in your church who are not involved in groups?

This survey has been written for churchwide use—in hopes that you may be able to rewrite it and use it in your own church. The courses described in this survey are taken from the present Serendipity 101, 201 and 301 courses for small groups.

Churchwide Survey for Small Groups

Name_____Phone_____

Section 1: Interest in Shared-Experience Groups

A shared-experience group is short-term in nature (7–13 weeks) and brings people together based on a common interest, experience or need in their lives. The various topics being considered for shared-experience groups are listed below.

1. Which of these shared-experience courses might be of interest to you? Check all that apply in the grid below under question 1 (Q1).

2. Which of these shared-experience groups would you be interested in hosting or co-leading? Check all that apply in the grid below under question 2 (Q2).

3. Which of these shared-experience groups do you think would be of interest to a friend or relative of yours who is on the fringe of the church? Check all that apply in the grid below under question 3 (Q3).

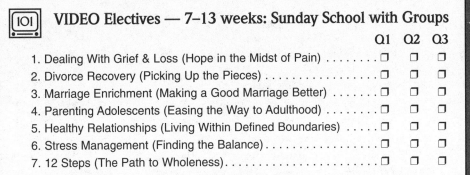

|101| **VIDEO Electives — 7–13 weeks: Sunday School with Groups**

	Q1	Q2	Q3
1. Dealing With Grief & Loss (Hope in the Midst of Pain)	☐	☐	☐
2. Divorce Recovery (Picking Up the Pieces)	☐	☐	☐
3. Marriage Enrichment (Making a Good Marriage Better)	☐	☐	☐
4. Parenting Adolescents (Easing the Way to Adulthood)	☐	☐	☐
5. Healthy Relationships (Living Within Defined Boundaries)	☐	☐	☐
6. Stress Management (Finding the Balance)	☐	☐	☐
7. 12 Steps (The Path to Wholeness)	☐	☐	☐

Survey The Needs —

 BEGINNER Bible Study — 7- to 13-week groups

	Q1	Q2	Q3
8. Stressed Out (Keeping Your Cool)	☐	☐	☐
9. Core Values (Setting My Moral Compass)	☐	☐	☐
10. Marriage (Seasons of Growth)	☐	☐	☐
11. Jesus (Up Close & Personal)	☐	☐	☐
12. Gifts & Calling (Discovering God's Will)	☐	☐	☐
13. Relationships (Learning to Love)	☐	☐	☐
14. Assessment (Personal Audit)	☐	☐	☐
15. Family (Stages of Parenting)	☐	☐	☐
16. Wholeness (Time for a Checkup)	☐	☐	☐
17. Beliefs (Basic Christianity)	☐	☐	☐

 DEEPER Bible Study — Varying Length Courses

	Q1	Q2	Q3
18. Supernatural: Amazing Stories (Jesus' Miracles) 13 wks.	☐	☐	☐
19. Discipleship: In His Steps (Life of Christ) 13 wks.	☐	☐	☐
20. Wisdom: The Jesus Classics (Jesus' Parables) 13 wks.	☐	☐	☐
21. Challenge: Attitude Adjustment (Sermon on the Mount) 13 wks.	☐	☐	☐
22. Endurance: Running the Race (Philippians) 11 wks.	☐	☐	☐
23. Teamwork: Together in Christ (Ephesians) 12 wks.	☐	☐	☐
24. Integrity: Taking on Tough Issues (1 Corinthians) 12–23 wks.	☐	☐	☐
25. Gospel: Jesus of Nazareth (Gospel of Mark) 13–26 wks.	☐	☐	☐
26. Leadership: Passing the Torch (1 & 2 Timothy) 14 wks.	☐	☐	☐
27. Excellence: Mastering the Basics (Romans) 15–27 wks.	☐	☐	☐
28. Hope: Looking at the End of Time (Revelation) 13–26 wks.	☐	☐	☐
29. Faithfulness: Walking in the Light (1 John) 11 wks.	☐	☐	☐
30. Freedom: Living by Grace (Galatians) 13 wks.	☐	☐	☐
31. Perseverance: Staying the Course (1 Peter) 10 wks.	☐	☐	☐
32. Performance: Faith at Work (James) 12 wks.	☐	☐	☐

DEPTH Bible Study — 13-week groups

	Q1	Q2	Q3
33. Ephesians (Our Riches in Christ)	☐	☐	☐
34. James (Walking the Talk)	☐	☐	☐
35. Life of Christ (Behold the Man)	☐	☐	☐
36. Miracles (Signs and Wonders)	☐	☐	☐
37. Parables (Virtual Reality)	☐	☐	☐
38. Philippians (Joy Under Stress)	☐	☐	☐
39. Sermon on the Mount (Examining Your Life)	☐	☐	☐
40. 1 John (The Test of Faith)	☐	☐	☐

Section 2: Covenant Groups (Long-term)

A covenant group is longer term (like an extended family), starting with a commitment for 7–13 weeks, with an option of renewing your covenant for the rest of the year. A covenant group can decide to change the topics they study over time. The general themes for the covenant groups that our church is considering are listed on the previous two pages.

4. Which of the following long-term covenant groups would you be interested in?

❏ Singles   ❏ Men   ❏ Women

❏ Couples   ❏ Parents   ❏ Downtown

❏ Twenty-Something   ❏ Thirty-Something   ❏ Empty Nesters

❏ Mixed   ❏ Breakfast   ❏ Engineers

❏ Young Marrieds   ❏ Seniors   ❏ Sunday Brunch

Section 3: Pre-Covenant Groups (Short-term)

To give you a taste of a small group, our church is offering a 7-week "trial" program for groups. For this trial program, the group will use the course ***Beginnings: A Taste of Serendipity.***

5. Would you be interested in joining a "trial" group?

❏ Yes   ❏ No   ❏ Maybe

6. What would be the most convenient time and place for you to meet?

❏ Weekday morning   ❏ At church

❏ Weekday evening   ❏ In a home

❏ Saturday morning

❏ Sunday after church

7. What kind of group would you prefer?

❏ Men

❏ Women

❏ Singles

❏ Couples

❏ Mixed

❏ Parents

❏ Seniors

❏ Around my age

❏ Doesn't matter

SERENDIPITY

BEGINNINGS

A TASTE OF SERENDIPITY

7 Sessions To Become
A Great Small Group!

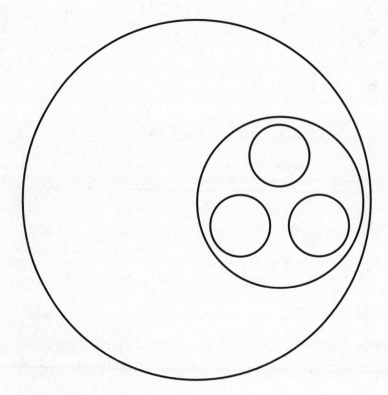

Step 4

Brainstorming

What did you learn about your church from the survey?

The Itch: Debrief together what you discovered from the survey about the need for small groups in your church. To begin with, find out in your group who checked Q3 for any of the 101 Video and 101 Beginner Electives (courses 1–17). Jot down in the box below the top three courses that you checked for 1–17.

Top Three Courses:

The Nitch: For the top three courses in the box above, find out if anyone in your group checked Q2 for these courses—i.e., that they would be willing to host or help lead a group that was interested in this course. Jot down the names of those in your group who checked Q2 in the box below.

Potential Hosts and Leaders:

The Apprentice / Leader and Leadership Core: Now, as a group, look over the names of the potential hosts and leaders you put in the box above and try to discern the person on this list who you think could easily be the leader of this new group, and one or two others who might fill out the Leadership Core for this new group. Jot down these names in the box below.

Apprentice / Leader and Leadership Core:

Q&A

What is the purpose of Covenant Groups?*

The members of the Covenant Group come together for the purpose of helping each other to:

* *Love God with all their heart, soul, mind and strength (Mark 12:30).*
* *Love their neighbors as themselves (Mark 12:31).*
* *Make disciples (Matthew 28:19).*

What are the qualifications of a Covenant Group leader?

A Covenant Group leader functions as a lay pastor, taking on himself or herself the responsibility of providing the primary care for the members of the group. Therefore, a Covenant Group leader exemplifies the following characteristics:

* *believes in Jesus Christ as their Lord and Savior*
* *has been a Christian for a while*
* *continues to grow in their faith*
* *cares for the well-being of others*
* *is able to set goals and work toward them*
* *demonstrates moral integrity*
* *listens to others*
* *is empathetic*
* *is willing to learn from others*
* *demonstrates flexibility*
* *respects others*
* *senses a call to serve*

A Covenant Group leader is not a perfect person! He or she need not know everything about leading and caring for others. Skills valuable to the role of a leader will be taught throughout the year, and care for the leader will be provided on an ongoing basis through a coach.

A Covenant Group leader is not necessarily a teacher. It is far more important that the leader be able to shepherd and care for the others in the group. Teaching is often a shared responsibility among group members.

---

* These four pages (M20–M23) are taken from the Training Manual For Group Leaders at Zionsville Presbyterian Church, Zionsville, IN, and are used by permission.

Questions & Answers

What does the church expect of a Covenant Group leader?

Every leader is asked to agree to the terms of the leader's covenant. Covenant Group leaders are to attend the monthly STP (Sharing, Training and Prayer) meeting. This gathering is held for the purposes of training and supporting leaders. The meeting takes place on the third Tuesday of each month, from 6:45 p.m. to 8:30 p.m. The two main elements of the STP event concern communication. The first half of the evening is devoted to disseminating the vision. The second half of the meeting consists of leaders huddling with their coach and with each other for the purpose of learning from one another. If a leader is unable to attend this meeting for some significant reason, he or she is to arrange another time to meet with their coach.

Leaders are also to fill out the Group Leader's Summary after every group event. This one-page reporting form takes only 10 minutes or so to complete and is a vital communication link between the staff liaison, the coach and the leader.

What can a Covenant Group leader expect in the way of support from the church?

A Covenant Group leader can expect the session and the staff to hold to the terms laid out in the Church's Covenant.

Every leader will be given a coach. This coach is someone whose ministry is to care for up to five leaders. The coach is charged with the responsibility of resourcing, encouraging, supporting, evaluating, challenging, loving and listening to the leaders in his or her care.

Every coach is supported by a staff member. If leaders ever have a situation where they feel that their coach is unable to help them, the staff liaison is there to be of assistance.

What is the role of a Covenant Group leader?

When people come together in groups, the group itself becomes an entity that is greater than the sum of its parts. The Covenant Group leader watches over the life and health of this new entity.

Specifically the Covenant Group leader is to:

- *find an apprentice*
- *pray and prepare for group meetings*
- *notify their coach or staff of acute crisis conditions requiring response*
- *develop and maintain an atmosphere in which members of the group can discover and develop God-given spiritual gifts*
- *pray for the spiritual growth and protection of each member*
- *refer counseling cases that exceed experience level*
- *convene the group two to four times each month*
- *recruit a host/hostess, when appropriate, and to see that child care and refreshments are available and a venue is arranged*
- *develop a healthy balance of love, learn, do, decide*
- *assure God's redemptive agenda via Scripture, sharing, prayers, songs and worship*
- *assist the group in refraining from divisiveness or teachings contrary to church position*
- *accept responsibility for group growth through the open-chair strategy*
- *lead an exemplary life*
- *regularly touch base with members outside the context of the group meeting just to say "Hi" and to see how they are doing*
- *help the group form a covenant and to review the covenant periodically*

While the Covenant Group leader takes primary responsibility for these activities, he or she should involve members of the group in many of them.

Does a Covenant Group really have to have a leader?

Yes! Without a leader a Covenant Group is like a ship at sea with no captain. A ship without a captain is at the mercy of the prevailing current and is unable to prepare for what may lie ahead. However, a ship with a captain has her course mapped out, and there is always someone at the helm ready to respond if necessary. So it is with a Covenant Group. The leader serves the others in the group by working to chart the best course as they together pursue being God's people on earth.

What are the critical elements of a Covenant Group?

A Covenant Group needs to have:

- *a leader*
- *an apprentice / leader*
- *members*

- *an open chair*
- *a covenant (see page M32)*

What is an Apprentice / Leader and how do we find one?

An apprentice / leader is someone who agrees that in time he or she will step out into leadership. Historically churches have tended to ask only those who aggressively step forward to serve in leadership positions. Rarely have churches worked at developing leaders. The result has been that most churches experience the phenomenon where only 20% of the congregation does 80% of the work. This historical approach stifles the giftedness of 80% of the church's population! In addition, the church has burned out many of their stand-out leaders by asking them to lead too many programs and too many people. Without some form of apprentice / leadership development, the church is constrained to overload its highly motivated, "here-I-am-send-me" leaders. The apprentice / leader model is meant to address these concerns.

The apprentice / leader is not an assistant. An assistant seldom has plans of stepping into the leader's shoes. Instead, the apprentice / leader works alongside the leader, with the intent of one day becoming a leader themselves. Along the way he or she is experiencing on-the-job training, learning the skills necessary to serve a small group as its leader.

It is the responsibility of the leader to find an apprentice / leader. The most important tools for the leader in this process are prayer and observation. The leader should pray, asking God to send someone whom he or she could mentor and train as a leader. Accompanying these prayers should be efforts to observe those who demonstrate signs of giftedness in shepherding, organizing, listening and faith. The one who is on time and who routinely prepares diligently for the group could be a candidate. The leader could also begin using the time before and after worship services, as well as various fellowship and educational events, to meet others in the congregation. As relationships are established, and the extent of a leader's acquaintances are broadened, the opportunity for finding a suitable apprentice / leader increases.

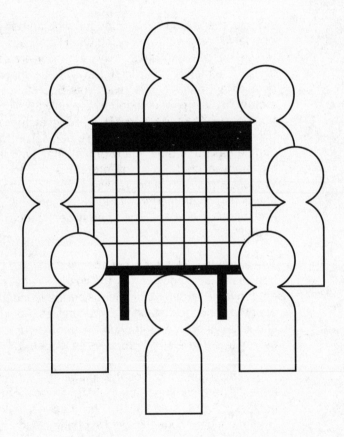

Step 5 Barnstorming

Who are you going to invite?

In the previous step, you identified the Apprentice / Leader and one or two others in your group who are going to be the leadership cell or core to start a new group.

Now, as a whole group, spend a few minutes creating a prospect list of people you would like to invite into this new group. Ask someone in your group to be the secretary and write down in the boxes below the names of people who come to mind:

Friends: Who are your friends in the church who you think might be interested in a small group?

Affinity: What are the special interests of the people in your leadership cell and who are the people in your church with the same interests? For instance, if the people in your leadership cell love tennis, who are the people in your church who might be interested in a small group before tennis? What about book lovers, entrepreneurs, empty nesters, senior citizens, stock watchers, etc.?

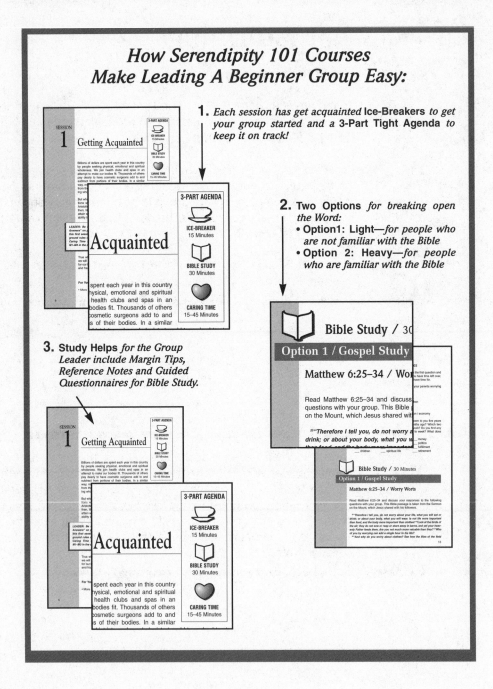

How Serendipity 101 Courses Make Leading A Beginner Group Easy:

1. *Each session has get acquainted* **Ice-Breakers** *to get your group started and a* **3-Part Tight Agenda** *to keep it on track!*

2. **Two Options** *for breaking open the Word:*
- **Option1: Light**—*for people who are not familiar with the Bible*
- **Option 2: Heavy**—*for people who are familiar with the Bible*

3. **Study Helps** *for the Group Leader include Margin Tips, Reference Notes and Guided Questionnaires for Bible Study.*

Who Do We Invite?

Felt Needs: Who are the people you know with the same felt needs? These people might be on the fringe of the church or even outside of the church. Go back to the survey on pages M15–M16 (the 101 courses) and think of people you feel could be hot prospects. For instance, who would be interested in "Stressed Out," "Marriage," "Wholeness," "Healthy Relationships," "Parenting Adolescents," etc.?

Geographical Location: Where do the people in your leadership team live or work, and who are the people in your church in the same area?

The Four Circles: Now, on this diagram, pinpoint the people you have jotted down in the four circles. Do you have any people on this list from the **Crowd** (the church dropouts)? Do you have anyone on your list from the **Community** (who do not attend any church)? It's really important that you have people from all four circles on your list.

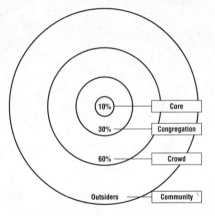

Step 6 Commissioning

Congratulations. You deserve a party.

Only two things remain for you to decide: (1) How are you going to commission the leadership team for the new group and (2) What is the rest of your group going to do next?

Going-away party

You have several options. If the church is planning a church-wide event for all of the groups (such as a graduation banquet), you would have a table at this event for your group. If your church is not planning an event, you must plan your own going-away party.

At this party, you may want to reminisce about your life together as a group with the questions below, have fun making some "Wild Predictions" (see page M30), share a Bible Study time (see page M31), and conclude with a time of commissioning and prayer.

Reminiscing Questions

1. What do you remember about the first time you attended this group?

2. How did you feel about opening up in this group and sharing your story?

3. What was the funniest thing that happened in this group?

4. What was the high point for you in this group?

5. What will you miss most about this group?

6. How would you like this group to stay in touch with each other after you multiply?

7. How did this group contribute to your life?

8. What is the biggest change that has occurred in your life since joining this group?

Wild Predictions

Try to match the people in your group to the crazy forecasts below. (Don't take it too seriously; it's meant to be fun!) Read out loud the first item and ask everyone to call out the name of the person who is most likely to accomplish this feat. Then, read the next item and ask everyone to make a new prediction, etc.

THE PERSON IN OUR GROUP MOST LIKELY TO ...

Make a million selling Beanie Babies over the Internet

Become famous for designing new attire for sumo wrestlers

Replace Vanna White on *Wheel of Fortune*

Appear on *The Tonight Show* to exhibit an acrobatic talent

Move to a desert island

Discover a new use for underarm deodorant

Succeed David Letterman as host of *The Late Show*

Substitute for John Madden as Fox's football color analyst

Appear on the cover of *Muscle & Fitness Magazine*

Become the newest member of the Spice Girls

Work as a bodyguard for Rush Limbaugh at Feminist convention

Write a best-selling novel based on their love life

Be a dance instructor on a cruise ship for wealthy, well-endowed widows

Win the blue ribbon at the state fair for best Rocky Mountain oyster recipe

Land a job as head librarian for Amazon.com

Be the first woman to win the Indianapolis 500

Open the Clouseau Private Detective Agency

Reflection Bible Study

Barnabas and Saul Sent Off — Acts 13:1–3, NIV

13 *In the church at Antioch there were prophets and teachers: Barnabas, Simeon called Niger, Lucius of Cyrene, Manaen (who had been brought up with Herod the tetrarch) and Saul. ²While they were worshiping the Lord and fasting, the Holy Spirit said, "Set apart for me Barnabas and Saul for the work to which I have called them." ³So after they had fasted and prayed, they placed their hands on them and sent them off.*

1. Why do you think God chose this small group in Antioch to launch the first missionary journey (instead of the church headquarters in Jerusalem)?
   ❏ It was merely coincidental.
   ❏ They were following the leading of the Holy Spirit.
   ❏ They were a bunch of outcasts from the fringe of the church.
   ❏ They didn't know how to "paint inside the lines."

2. How do you think the leadership back in Jerusalem felt when they heard what these guys were doing?
   ❏ thrilled   ❏ angry that they didn't follow protocol
   ❏ embarrassed   ❏ They probably didn't hear about it until later.

3. Why do you think the small group chose two people to send out instead of one?
   ❏ for companionship
   ❏ They had different gifts: Paul was a hothead, Barnabas an encourager.
   ❏ It was coincidental.

4. As you think about sending out some members of your small group to give "birth" to a new group, what is your greatest concern for these people?
   ❏ keeping the faith   ❏ keeping their personal walk with Christ
   ❏ keeping the vision   ❏ keeping in touch with us for support

5. As one who is going to lead or colead a new group, how would you describe your emotions right now?
   ❏ a nervous wreck   ❏ delivery room jitters
   ❏ pregnant with excitement   ❏ Ask me next week.

6. If you could say one word of encouragement to those who are going to be new leaders, what would it be?
   ❏ I'll be praying for you.   ❏ You can do it.
   ❏ Call me anytime.   ❏ It's okay to fail.

What do we do next?

For those who are going to stay with the "mother group," you need to decide on your new covenant and who you are going to invite to fill the empty chairs left by the departing "missionaries."

Do we ever meet again?

Definitely! Plan NOW for "homecoming" next year when the new group returns for a time of celebration. Four good times: the World Series, Super Bowl, Final Four and Stanley Cup.

Group Covenant

Any group can benefit from creating or renewing a group covenant. Take some time for those remaining in the "mother group" to discuss the following questions. When everyone in the group has the same expectations for the group, everything runs more smoothly.

1. The purpose of our group is:

2. The goals of our group are:

3. We will meet for _____ weeks, after which we will decide if we wish to continue as a group. If we do decide to continue, we will reconsider this covenant.

4. We will meet _____ (weekly, every other week, monthly).

5. Our meetings will be from _____ o'clock to _____ o'clock, and we will strive to start and end on time.

6. We will meet at _____ or rotate from house to house.

7. We will take care of the following details: ❏ child care ❏ refreshments

8. We agree to the following rules for our group:

   ❏ PRIORITY: While we are in this group, group meetings have priority.

   ❏ PARTICIPATION: Everyone is given the right to their own opinion and all questions are respected.

   ❏ CONFIDENTIALITY: Anything said in the meeting is not to be repeated outside the meeting.

   ❏ EMPTY CHAIR: The group stays open to new people and invites prospective members to visit the group.

   ❏ SUPPORT: Permission is given to call each other in times of need.

   ❏ ADVICE GIVING: Unsolicited advice is not allowed.

   ❏ MISSION: We will do everything in our power to start a new group.

3. Contrast verse 6 with 2:12. What has changed because of what Christ has done?

4. From verses 7–9, what can you learn about Paul? About God?

Paul

God

5. In your own words, how would you explain the mission of the church from verses 6,10–11?

6. What are the practical benefits of being in Christ (vv. 12–13)?

APPLY
The Gospel, while intensely personal, has broad social effects. In our day, what parallels to the first century's tensions over Jews and Gentiles do you see (example: pro-life vs. pro-choice advocates; labor vs. management, etc.)?

Since Gentiles and Jews were to be seen as "heirs together" (v. 6), what does this imply about how you ought to relate to those who are on the "wrong side" of the issues that are important to you?

In what ways does this especially challenge you now?

GROUP AGENDA

After the first part, read the Scripture out loud and divide into groups of 4. Then come back together for the third part.

TO BEGIN / 10–15 Min. (Choose 1 or 2)

1. Where was your secret hiding place when you were a child?

2. Who is your favorite mystery writer, or your favorite mystery on TV or in the movies?

3. If you could take the Gospel to people of another country or to a group of people in your own country, where would you go?

TO GO DEEPER / 30 Min. (Choose 2 or 3)

1. What exactly is the mystery that Paul is referring to (second question in SEARCH)?

2. Do you think Paul was putting himself down when he called himself "less than the least" of all God's people? Or was he just being appropriately humble?

3. What are your thoughts in the APPLY section?

4. What types of people would feel excluded from your church? What can you do about that?

5. How would you compare Paul's passion to share the "mystery" of the Gospel to your own spiritual passion?

6. CASE STUDY: Carolyn says, "Who needs the church anyway? It's boring, and just doesn't seem to have anything to offer me. I worship God better on my own." Using this passage, how would you broaden Carolyn's perspective? What practical help might you give her to address her feelings?

TO CLOSE / 15–30 Min.

1. Are you thinking and dreaming about your group's mission? (See center section.)

2. On a scale of 1 (low) to 10 (high), with how much "freedom and confidence" (v. 12) do you approach God?

3. How can the group pray for you?

NOTES

Summary. This section is divided into two parts. First, Paul describes in verses 1–6 how he came to grasp the truth that Jew and Gentile are one in Christ (by revelation). Then, second, he explains in verses 7–13 how he came to preach this truth. Both his understanding of this mystery and his call to preach it are the result of "God's grace that was given to me." This phrase is used in verse 2 and in verse 7 by way of introduction to each theme.

3:1 *For this reason.* Paul continues to write in the same ragged fashion characteristic of one who is dictating to a scribe. The letter to the Ephesians is not a carefully crafted composition which has gone through a series of drafts and an editorial committee. Here in verse 1, Paul breaks off his prayer in midstride. He mentions the Gentiles and it strikes him that he ought to say a word about how he came to be their apostle. He will pick up his prayer again in verse 14.

prisoner. It is quite possible (though not certain) that Paul was under house arrest and not in a prison cell. He was probably in a rented home. He was able to read and write, and to receive visitors. However, he was chained day and night to one of a series of Roman soldiers. In 6:20 he calls himself "an ambassador in chains."

the prisoner of Christ Jesus. He was, in fact, Nero's prisoner. But Paul knows better. Nero may have the power to incarcerate him, but it is Jesus who commands his love, allegiance and freely given service.

for the sake of you Gentiles. This statement is literally true. Paul was in prison awaiting trial precisely because of his ministry to the Gentiles. He was arrested in the first place because it was thought he had brought Gentiles into the temple in Jerusalem (Acts 21:27–32; 22:22–29). Throughout his ministry, his claim that God was creating a new people which included Gentiles on an equal basis with Jews aroused severe opposition. The vision he presented in chapter 2 is the cause of his suffering.

3:2 *Surely you have heard.* Paul could not say this to people who knew him as well as the people in Ephesus. They knew beyond a doubt that God had revealed to Paul that Jew and Gentile are one in Christ and that Paul was called to preach this message. Paul's use of this phrase seems to argue that this letter was intended for a wider audience than just the church at Ephesus.

3:3 *mystery.* In English this word has the sense of something which is hidden and perhaps even incomprehensible. In Greek, a mystery is something that, while it is beyond human reason to figure it out, once revealed by God it is open and plain to all. This is a key word in this passage.

revelation. This new reality is not something Paul figured out on his own; nor was it the product of a theological committee. It was given by God.

3:5 *not made known to men in other generations.* In the Old Testament it was clear that the Gentiles would one day be blessed through Abraham (Gen. 12:1–3; Psalm 2:8; Isa. 2:2–4; 42:6–7; 49:6). In the New Testament, Jesus told his disciples to make disciples of all nations (Matt. 28:19). But what had not yet been made clear was the radical nature of God's intention: the complete union of both Jew and Gentile in Christ given concrete expression in a new body, the church.

revealed ... to God's holy apostles and prophets. It was not only to Paul that God revealed this new truth about the Gentiles. In Acts 10:9–23, Peter learns by means of a divine vision that Gentiles are no longer to be considered impure and outside God's kingdom.

3:6 *heirs together / members together / sharers together.* Paul's point is that these two groups— once traditional enemies—now share together the same promised covenant blessings, the same body and the same benefits.

3:7 *this gospel.* The mystery revealed to Paul now becomes the message preached by Paul.

by the gift of God's grace. In the same way that the mystery was revealed to Paul "by grace" (v. 2), so too his call to preach is also by grace.

working of his power. Here is another example of God's astonishing power. Paul, who killed Christians, has been transformed by that power into one who creates Christians (by preaching the Gospel). The two "power" words used here are (in root form) *energeia* and *dunamis* (see note on 1:19).

3:8 *less than the least.* Paul invents yet another Greek word! Taking a superlative meaning "least" or "smallest" he alters it (although grammatically it is impossible to do so) so that it becomes a comparative meaning "leaster" or "less than the least." There is probably also some wordplay going on here. Paul's Roman name *Paulus* means "little." This is no

mere word game, however. Paul really feels this way about himself, probably because he once persecuted the church (1 Cor. 15:9; Gal. 1:13). It is important to note, however, that while Paul may downplay himself, he never demeans the authority of his office as an apostle. In 4:1, for example, Paul uses the apostolic "I." He is not afraid to speak with direct authority.

riches. Paul has named these riches in chapters 1 and 2. These include: redemption (1:7); forgiveness of sins (1:7); knowledge of his will (1:9–10); an inheritance (1:14,18); power (1:19); resurrection with Christ (2:5–6); enthronement with Christ (2:6); grace (2:7); kindness (2:7); citizenship in God's kingdom (2:19); and membership in God's family (2:19).

3:9 *to make plain.* In Greek this verb is *photizo*, from which "photo" and "photography" are derived. It means "to enlighten." By it Paul focuses on the condition of the lost (they are in darkness). Paul's original commission, given by Jesus on the Damascus Road, carried this idea: "I am sending you to open their eyes and turn them from darkness to light ..." (Acts 26:17–18).

everyone. Paul's ministry involves not just the evangelism of the Gentiles but also the enlightenment of all people as to God's intention.

3:10 *manifold.* This word means, literally, "multicolored." It was used to describe the riot of color found in a Greek flower garden or in an intricate pattern of embroidered cloth. This is a fitting image for the multicolored, multinational, multiethnic church, newly forged in Jesus Christ.

made known to the rulers and authorities in the heavenly realms. At this point Paul's vision soars to new heights as he declares that it is by means of this multiethnic church that the very supernatural powers themselves see what God is up to in the universe. They watch in fascination as traditional enemies (Jews and Gentiles) are drawn together into the church and by this they learn about "the manifold wisdom of God."

3:12 *we may approach God.* Another facet of this new reality is the fact that all people may now approach God. No longer is it necessary to come to him via a priest or other mediator. The sixteenth-century Reformers labeled this doctrine the "priesthood of all believers."

UNIT 7—A Prayer for the Ephesians / Eph. 3:14-21

A Prayer for the Ephesians

¹⁴For this reason I kneel before the Father, ¹⁵from whom his whole family ª in heaven and on earth derives its name. ¹⁶I pray that out of his glorious riches he may strengthen you with power through his Spirit in your inner being, ¹⁷so that Christ may dwell in your hearts through faith. And I pray that you, being rooted and established in love, ¹⁸may have power, together with all the saints, to grasp how wide and long and high and deep is the love of Christ, ¹⁹and to know this love that surpasses knowledge—that you may be filled to the measure of all the fullness of God.

²⁰Now to him who is able to do immeasurably more than all we ask or imagine, according to his power that is at work within us, ²¹to him be glory in the church and in Christ Jesus throughout all generations, for ever and ever! Amen.

ª15 Or *whom all fatherhood*

READ

First Reading / First Impressions: How do you sense Paul prayed this prayer?

❏ mechanically everyday

❏ joyfully, probably singing at the end

❏ quietly, to keep up his image in front of the guards

Second Reading / Big Idea: The basic request Paul makes in this prayer is:

SEARCH

1. What are the three specific requests that Paul makes (see "Summary" in the notes)?

> vv. 16–17a

> vv. 17b–19a

> v. 19b

2. Request #1: What is the means by which this power comes? What is its result?

3. Request #2: What two things does Paul desire for us? Who is with us in this? How does this relate to Paul's vision in 1:9–10?

4. Request #3: In your own words, how would you express what Paul desires for all of us?

APPLY

Using Paul's prayer in this passage as a model, write a prayer for yourself.

For example, "God, I bow before you because ..."

"I pray for your strength so that ..."

"I pray that I might grasp or understand ..."

Secondly, think of someone you are concerned about. In light of Paul's prayer here, write a prayer for them.

For example, "God, I pray that _____ would have your strength / understanding to ..."

This would be a wonderful portion of Scripture to memorize. Give some consideration, perhaps as a group project, to memorizing this passage for ongoing reflection.

GROUP AGENDA

After the first part, read the Scripture out loud and divide into groups of 4. Then come back together for the third part.

TO BEGIN / 10–15 Min. (Choose 1 or 2)

1. When you were 12 years old, what did you want to be when you grew up?

2. Who had a great influence on your life when you were an adolescent?

3. When do you feel closest to God?

TO GO DEEPER / 30 Min. (Choose 2 or 3)

1. In the READ and SEARCH sections, what impressed you the most in answering the questions and reading the notes?

2. What would you expect to see happen in people for whom a prayer like this was being fulfilled?

3. What could you learn from Paul's prayer for your own prayer life?

4. What does your prayer life show about what you think about God?

5. CASE STUDY: Several years ago you were in a prayer group that concentrated on praise to God for a long time together. Now, you are more occupied with problems and daily needs. What happened?

TO CLOSE / 15–30 Min.

1. Are you happy with your group's progress on developing your mission?

2. Share one of the prayers you wrote in the APPLY section.

3. What is the biggest thing you have asked God for in the last week? Month? Year?

4. Where do you need the power of God to work in your life right now? How can this group join you in prayer?

NOTES

Summary. This section has been called "one of the gems of the epistle" (Mitton) and "the highlight of Ephesians" (Haupt). In it Paul completes the prayer he began in 3:1. In the prayer itself (vv. 16–19), Paul asks for two main things—strength and knowledge—via three petitions. In verses 16–17a Paul asks that Christians be given inner strength. In verses 17b–19a he asks that they might know God's will (and especially know about Christ's love). In verse 19b he asks that Christians be perfected. In these three sections, he prays "for the work of the Spirit, the presence of Christ, and the manifestation of God's glory in the saints" (Barth). The focus of 3:14–21 is on the individual believer and their ongoing experience of the triune God. This emphasis on the individual balances nicely the previous emphasis (2:11–3:13) on the collective (the church). Being a Christian involves both individual growth and collective community.

3:14–19 In Greek this is all one sentence.

3:14 *For this reason.* Paul repeats this phrase, first used in 3:1, and so picks up again the prayer he began back there. What motivates this prayer and shapes its content is what he said in chapters 1 and 2. There he pointed out God's intention to create a new body (the church) out of old enemies (Jew and Gentile). To be a part of such a company is humanly impossible—unless a person is changed from within. So this is what Paul will pray for. He will pray that God the Holy Spirit will work in their inner being (v. 16); that God the Son will dwell in their hearts (v. 17); and that God the Father will fill them with his fullness (v. 19).

I kneel. Jews typically stood when they prayed as is seen in the Parable of the Pharisee and the Tax Collector (Luke 18:9–14; see also Matthew 6:5 and Mark 11:25). However, in times of great distress and deep feeling one might kneel or lie prostrate. Ezra did this when he heard about the intermarriage between the people of Israel and the surrounding tribes (Ezra 9:3–5). In Gethsemane Jesus "fell with his face to the ground and prayed" (Matt. 26:39).

Father. Paul seems to intend this title to have cosmic significance. God is the Father over all, whether they yet know him or not. In 4:6 he will call him "Father of all, who is over all and through all and in all." Thus, in the same way that in 1:4–23 Paul describes Christ in cosmic terms, so here he describes the Father in the same way.

3:15 *family.* There may be some wordplay going on here. "Father" in Greek is *pater* and "family" is *patria*. This is a family derived from the Father.

in heaven and on earth. There are two parts to God's family: those on earth ("the church militant") and those in heaven ("the church triumphant").

name. In the early centuries, the act of naming was far more significant than merely giving a child a label to distinguish him or her from other children. To be named was to be given an identity and purpose. To be called by God's name is to be put under God's power and protection.

3:16 *strengthen you with power.* Paul asks that Christians be fortified or invigorated within by the Holy Spirit. He asks that they experience this awesome power of God about which he has written so eloquently. Having been empowered, then they are able to grasp the awesome love God has for them (v. 19). Inner power makes inner knowledge possible.

inner being. By this term Paul may be referring to the deepest part of the human personality where a person's true essence lies. The Greeks thought that there were three parts to one's inner being: reason—by which a person discerns right; conscience—as a result of which a person strives for purity and holiness; and will—from which that person derives the ability to do what they know to be right. Furthermore it would appear that it is via one's inner being that God is experienced. The Holy Spirit moves in power there. Christ dwells there. God the Father works there (vv. 19–20).

3:17 *dwell.* There are two Greek words which can be used to describe taking up residency. The first, *paroikeo,* means "to inhabit (a place) as a stranger" or "to live as a stranger" (Bauer). Paul uses this word in 2:19 where it is translated "aliens." The second word, which is used here, *katoikeo,* means "to settle down" or "to dwell" and it implies a permanent residency (in a house) as against a temporary stopover (in a tent). In other words, Christ has come to stay. In Colossians 1:27, Paul states that part of this mystery which has been now revealed is that Christ dwells within us.

faith. This is the means by which a person is open to the indwelling Christ.

rooted and established. By his choice of these words Paul hints at two metaphors through which the character of love is revealed. The Christian is to be anchored firmly in the soil of love just like a tree. The Christian is also to be set solidly on the foundation of love just like a well-constructed house. (The second word in Greek is literally "grounded.")

love. *Agape* love is selfless giving to others regardless of how one feels. Such love is the foundation upon which the church will grow. Otherwise the newly redeemed enemies would remain enemies.

3:18 *power.* Not only does the Christian need power in order to love but a Christian needs power even to comprehend the love of Christ.

together with all the saints. Knowing the love of Christ is vital for the whole church. Christ's love cannot, by definition, be known in isolation. Love, to be love, must be experienced and expressed. Love is the fuel by which the church is sustained and grows.

wide / long / high / deep. Paul struggles to express the magnitude of God's love. "Modern commentators warn us not to be too literal in our interpretation of these, since the apostle may only have been indulging in a little rhetoric or poetic hyperbole. Yet it seems legitimate to say that the love of Christ is 'broad' enough to encompass all mankind (especially Jews and Gentiles, the theme of these chapters), 'long' enough to last for eternity, 'deep' enough to reach the most degraded sinner, and 'high' enough to exalt him to heaven" (Stott).

3:19 *to know this love that surpasses knowledge.* Again Paul uses extravagant language to make his point. He prays that they will know what can't be known! God's love is such that limited human faculties can never grasp its fullness (though Christians must strive to do so).

3:20 Paul prays because God is able to do what is asked. In fact, he is able to do much more than we can either ask or even imagine (think) because of his great power.

immeasurably more. Once again Paul coins his own word, in this case a "super-superlative" (Bruce) which is difficult to translate into English. J. B. Phillips renders this double-compound as "infinitely more." By this Paul intends to convey that given our limited knowledge, we cannot even pray for all that God can and will do for us.

his power that is at work within us. This power is within individual Christians and within the body as a whole. This is the power Paul has struggled all along to describe and explain.

UNIT 8—Unity in the Body of Christ / Eph. 4:1–16

Unity in the Body of Christ

4 As a prisoner for the Lord, then, I urge you to live a life worthy of the calling you have received. ²Be completely humble and gentle; be patient, bearing with one another in love. ³Make every effort to keep the unity of the Spirit through the bond of peace. ⁴There is one body and one Spirit—just as you were called to one hope when you were called—⁵one Lord, one faith, one baptism; ⁶one God and Father of all, who is over all and through all and in all.

⁷But to each one of us grace has been given as Christ apportioned it. ⁸This is why it[a] says:

> "When he ascended on high,
>   he led captives in his train
>   and gave gifts to men."[b]

⁹(What does "he ascended" mean except that he also descended to the lower, earthly regions[c]? ¹⁰He who descended is the very one who ascended higher than all the heavens, in order to fill the whole universe.) ¹¹It was he who gave some to be apostles, some to be prophets, some to be evangelists, and some to be pastors and teachers, ¹²to prepare God's people for works of service, so that the body of Christ may be built up ¹³until we all reach unity in the faith and in the knowledge of the Son of God and become mature, attaining to the whole measure of the fullness of Christ.

¹⁴Then we will no longer be infants, tossed back and forth by the waves, and blown here and there by every wind of teaching and by the cunning and craftiness of men in their deceitful scheming. ¹⁵Instead, speaking the truth in love, we will in all things grow up into him who is the Head, that is, Christ. ¹⁶From him the whole body, joined and held together by every supporting ligament, grows and builds itself up in love, as each part does its work.

[a]8 Or *God*   [b]8 Psalm 68:18   [c]9 Or *the depths of the earth*

READ

First Reading / First Impressions: Does this passage strike you more as an affirmation or rebuke?

Second Reading / Big Idea: What words or phrases seem to be central in this passage?

SEARCH

1. From 3:6, what is the "calling" (4:1) that Christians have received?

2. How would the qualities in verses 2–3 help the Christian live this call to unity (see notes)?

3. Although the church is to be unified, that does not mean we are all to be the same. What can you learn about the different gifts ("graces") in the church regarding:

their source (vv. 7–8)?

their purpose (vv. 12–14)?

4. As opposed to being "blown here and there" by deceitful people and teachings (v. 14), how would you paraphrase Paul's vision for the church in verses 15–16?

APPLY

The application exercises in this course have been primarily personal. Now think of the others in your group and "affirm" their gifts by pointing out to them the gifts ("graces") you see in their lives. Although Scripture mentions over 20 different gifts, four are stressed here (v. 11). See the notes for insight about their meaning. Then, jot down the initials of the others in your group next to the special gift you see in them. If none fit, what other gift do you see in that person?

Apostle: Originally meant "ambassador" for the king. Broadened to mean anyone who brings the Good News to an area—someone gifted with daring, vision and strong leadership.

Prophet: Originally meant "spokesman" for God in the Old Testament. Broadened to mean someone who speaks out for God on issues—gifted in courage, exhortation and admonition to the church and society.

Evangelist: Originally meant wandering storytellers. Broadened to mean someone who can make clear the Gospel message to outsiders—gifted in communication, witnessing and convincing.

Pastor / Teacher: In the original Greek, the gift is combined. Literally means shepherd to: (a) care for the needs of others and (b) preserve and protect the Christian tradition—gifted in sensitivity, compassion and deep insight.

Other:_____

GROUP AGENDA

After the first part, read the Scripture out loud and divide into groups of 4. Then come back together for the third part.

TO BEGIN / 10–15 Min. (Choose 1 or 2)

1. Who was, or is, the peacemaker in your family?

2. At what time in your life was your body in the best physical condition?

3. What is the most "together" group or team you have ever been a part of? What made this group so close?

TO GO DEEPER / 30 Min. (Choose 2 or 3)

1. If you have completed the homework, what stands out to you from READ or SEARCH?

2. From verses 1–3, what would you say was the problem with the church in Ephesus?

3. Of the qualities in verse 2, which one most needs developing in your life? Is there a particular relationship in which you need to apply this quality?

4. As opposed to love without truth or truth without love, what does it mean to "speak the truth in love" (v. 15)? How hard is it for you to do this?

5. CASE STUDY: Your friend grew up in a church where there were only two kinds of Christians: the ordained priesthood and everybody else. Your friend would like to be used by God, but does not feel called to the priesthood or ordination. What is your counsel?

6. A healthy body "grows and builds itself up in love, as each part does its work" (v. 16). How is your church doing in accomplishing this? Are you doing your part?

TO CLOSE / 15–30 Min.

1. Have one person at a time listen while others share the gift ("grace") they identified for that person in APPLY.

2. What can your group draw from this time of affirmation to help in calling a leadership team to start a new group?

3. How can the group pray for you?

NOTES

Summary. Paul begins the second half of his epistle by calling for all Christians to lead "a life worthy" of the grand plan they have been called to be part of. Thus he signals his shift in focus from *doctrine* (chapters 1–3) to *duty* (chapters 4–6); from *exposition* of the mystery of God to *exhortation* to live in a way that is consistent with what they now know to be true. Paul begins chapter 4 by focusing on those attitudes, actions and insights that foster unity within the body (vv. 1–6). Then he shifts his emphasis to the diversity of gifts and functions within the one body (vv. 7–13). He ends by pointing to the maturity produced by such diversity within unity (vv. 14–16).

4:1 *I urge you.* The first half of the book was a long prayer for the church and an exposition of how it was created. Now Paul, with the full weight of his apostolic authority ("I"), exhorts and beseeches all who are part of this church to live a new style of life. Having expounded what God did, he now explains what they must do. In other words, stylistically Paul moves from the indicative ("This is the way things are") to the imperative ("This is what must be done").

a life worthy. This is the theme of the remainder of Ephesians. Having described the creation by God of this new society, Paul now defines the lifestyle of this new race of people (Christians).

4:2 Paul identifies the five qualities of life that promote unity between people: humility, gentleness, patience, mutual forbearance and love.

humble. It is interesting that within Greek culture, humility was not seen as a virtue. Humility was viewed as cringing subservience and was despised. Christians came to understand humility in quite a different way. Humility was understood to be an absence of pride and self-assertion (both of which are sources of discord) based upon accurate self-knowledge and on an understanding of the God-given worth of others.

gentle. The RSV translates this word as "meekness." But Paul is not urging people to be timid and without convictions. Gentleness "is not a synonym for 'weakness.' On the contrary, it is the gentleness of the strong, whose strength is under control" (Stott).

be patient. Patience is "slowness in avenging wrong or retaliating when hurt by another" (Foulkes).

bearing with one another. This is the kind of tolerance of the faults of others which springs from humility, gentleness and patience.

4:3 *Make every effort.* What Paul is saying is: "Work zealously at maintaining in visible form what has already been achieved for you by Christ and is therefore a fact."

unity. This is what each of the virtues in verse 2 aim at: the close bonding of people to one another. While verse 4 indicates that what is in view is the unity of the Christian church, these same attitudes build unity in all kinds of relationships: within marriage, across generations, between groups.

the bond of peace. This peace has been made possible through Jesus Christ who first reconciled humanity to God (bringing peace with God) and then reconciled people to one another (creating a bond of peace between them).

4:4 *one.* It is very hard to miss Paul's stress on unity. He repeats the word "one" some seven times in three verses. In fact, given the rhythm and phrasing of verses 4–6, it seems likely that Paul is quoting an ancient Christian hymn, or a catechism.

4:7–13 From a discussion of unity (vv. 1–6) Paul turns here to a discussion of diversity. As he will show, unity does not mean uniformity.

4:7 *grace.* In 2:1–10, Paul discussed saving grace. Here his focus is on the grace by which these redeemed men and women serve Christ and his church (serving grace).

4:8 Paul quotes Psalm 68:18 which describes the triumphal procession of a conquering Jewish king up Mt. Zion and into Jerusalem. The king is followed by a procession of prisoners in chains. As he marches up the hill, he is given gifts of tribute and in turn disperses gifts of booty. Paul uses this verse to describe Christ's ascension into heaven. The captives which follow along behind him are the principalities and powers which he has defeated (see 1:20–22 and Col. 2:15). The gifts which the conquering Christ disperses are gifts of ministry given to his followers.

4:9 *descended.* Paul is referring to Christ's incarnation whereby he came down from heaven and invaded space and time (see Phil. 2:5–11). He may also be referring to Christ's death and subsequent invasion of hell (see 1 Pet. 3:19; 4:6).

4:11 This is one of several lists of gifts (see Rom. 12:6–8; 1 Cor. 12:8–10,28–30). No single list is exhaustive, defining all the gifts. Each is illustrative. The emphasis in this list is on teaching gifts.

apostles. Paul probably had in mind the small group of men who had seen the resurrected Christ and been commissioned by him to launch his church (see Acts 1:21–22; 1 Cor. 9:1). These would include the Twelve (1 Cor. 15:5) and a few others (e.g., Rom. 16:7). In this sense there are no longer any apostles, yet "it is certainly possible to argue that there are people with apostolic ministries of a different kind, including episcopal jurisdiction, pioneer missionary work, church planting, itinerant leadership, etc." (Stott).

prophets. In contrast to teachers who relied upon the Old Testament Scripture and the teaching of Jesus to instruct others, prophets offered words of instruction, exhortation and admonition which were immediate and unpremeditated. Their source was direct revelation from God. These prophecies were often directed to specific situations. At times, however, their words related to the future (Acts 11:27–28).

evangelists. In the early centuries of the church, these were the men and women who moved from place to place, telling the Gospel story to those who had not heard it and/or believed it. While all Christians are called upon to be witnesses of the Gospel, the reference here is to those with the special gift of evangelism. This gift is the ability to make the Gospel clear and convincing to many people.

pastors and teachers. The way in which this is expressed in Greek indicates that these two functions reside in one person. In a day when books were rare and expensive, it was the task of the pastor / teacher not only to look after the welfare of the flock (the title "pastor" means, literally, "shepherd") but to preserve the Christian tradition and instruct people in it.

4:12 *prepare.* These teaching gifts are to be used to train everyone in the church so that each Christian is capable of ministry. In other words, the prime task of the clergy is to train the laity to do ministry. This stands in contrast to many churches where the laity hire clergy to do ministry. In 3:12 Paul taught the concept of the "priesthood of all believers." Here he teaches "the ministry of all believers."

4:13–16 The aim of all these gifts is to produce maturity. Maturity is, in turn, vital to unity—the theme with which Paul began this section.

4:15 *speaking the truth in love.* Christians are to stand for both truth and love. Both are necessary. Truth without love becomes harsh. Love without truth becomes weak.

UNIT 9—Children of Light—Part 1 / Eph. 4:17–32

Living as Children of Light

¹⁷*So I tell you this, and insist on it in the Lord, that you must no longer live as the Gentiles do, in the futility of their thinking. ¹⁸They are darkened in their understanding and separated from the life of God because of the ignorance that is in them due to the hardening of their hearts. ¹⁹Having lost all sensitivity, they have given themselves over to sensuality so as to indulge in every kind of impurity, with a continual lust for more.*

²⁰*You, however, did not come to know Christ that way. ²¹Surely you heard of him and were taught in him in accordance with the truth that is in Jesus. ²²You were taught, with regard to your former way of life, to <u>put off your old self</u>, which is being corrupted by its deceitful desires; ²³to be made new in the attitude of your minds; ²⁴and to put on the new self, created to be like God in true righteousness and holiness.*

²⁵*Therefore each of you must put off falsehood and speak truthfully to his neighbor, for we* are all members of one body. ²⁶*"In your anger do not sin"ᵃ: Do not let the sun go down while you are still angry, ²⁷and do not give the devil a foothold. ²⁸He who has been stealing must steal no longer, but must work, doing something useful with his own hands, that he may have something to share with those in need.*

²⁹*Do not let any unwholesome talk come out of your mouths, but only what is helpful for building others up according to their needs, that it may benefit those who listen. ³⁰And do not grieve the Holy Spirit of God, with whom you were sealed for the day of redemption. ³¹Get rid of all bitterness, rage and anger, brawling and slander, along with every form of malice. ³²Be kind and compassionate to one another, forgiving each other, just as in Christ God forgave you.*

ᵃ26 Psalm 4:4

READ
First Reading / First Impressions: How many commands can you find in this passage?_____

Second Reading / Big Idea: In your own words, write out what seems to be the major command here for you.

SEARCH
1. How would you compare moral standards in Paul's day to our day?

2. As opposed to living in the "old way" (vv. 18–19), how would you explain what it means for you as a Christian to:

   put off your old self (v. 22)?

44

be made new in the attitude of your mind (v. 23)?

put on the new self, created to be like God (v. 24)?

3. How does Paul illustrate what this principle means in the following verses (see notes)?

OLD WAY	NEW WAY
(v. 25)	
(vv. 26–27)	
(v. 28)	
(v. 29)	
(vv. 30–32a)	

4. What motives for living in this new way does Paul give us (vv. 20–21,25b,32b)?

APPLY

Verses 31–32 give six negative qualities we are to get rid of and three positive qualities we are to cultivate. Examine your life on each of these qualities and put a dot on the line—somewhere between NO PROBLEM (left) and BIG PROBLEM (right)—to rate yourself on each of them.

	NO PROBLEM	BIG PROBLEM
Getting rid of all bitterness (holding a grudge)		
Getting rid of rage (pent-up hostile feelings)		
Getting rid of anger (explosive temper)		
Getting rid of brawling (loud-mouthed outburst)		
Getting rid of slander (insulting talk behind back)		
Getting rid of malice (plotting evil of another)		
Being kind (generous, quick to respond to need)		
Being compassionate (tender, sensitive, empathetic)		
Being forgiving (taking initiative to mend hurts)		

GROUP AGENDA

After the first part, read the Scripture out loud and divide into groups of 4. Then come back together for the third part.

TO BEGIN / 10–15 Min. (Choose 1 or 2)

1. When you were a child, did you have special "Sunday clothes" or "Sunday shoes"?

2. How old were you when your parents finally let you choose your own clothes?

3. Do you like dressing up or wearing old grubbies all the time?

4. What New Year's resolution have you been least successful in keeping?

TO GO DEEPER / 30 Min. (Choose 2 or 3)

1. If you've completed the homework, share your answer to a question you found interesting, helpful or especially meaningful.

✓ 2. Would Paul believe that it is possible to change conduct without a change of the heart ... or change the heart without a change in conduct?

✓ 3. Why are programs that emphasize "putting on" more popular than programs that emphasize "putting off"?

4. CASE STUDY: John, a Christian, is an active member of a local union which has been on a prolonged, bitter strike over what he considers legitimate grievances. Recently, tensions have mounted as some union members are suspected of having vandalized the home of one of the management personnel who lives near John. John knows other neighbors, not connected with the dispute, are going to help clean up the man's home. What should John do?

TO CLOSE / 15–30 Min.

1. Has your group assigned three people as a leadership core to start a new small group?

2. Where did you mark yourself strongest and weakest under APPLY on your worksheet?

3. Do you do better by concentrating on overcoming your weaknesses or by forgetting about them?

4. How can the group support you in prayer?

NOTES

Summary. Paul continues his exposition of the "life worthy of (our) calling" (4:1). Having urged the Christians to cultivate *unity* (4:1–16), now he urges them to cultivate *purity* (4:17–5:21). In shifting his topic, Paul shifts his focus. In discussing unity his focus was on the Christian community. In discussing purity his focus will be on the Christian individual.

4:17 *as the Gentiles do.* Paul begins this section on purity of life by describing the typical Gentile lifestyle from which Christians must flee. Not every Gentile lived this way, of course. Still, Paul's description of how they as pagans once lived is similar to what Gentile authors were saying. The Gentile lifestyle is described in a fashion parallel to Paul's more extended exposition in Romans 1:18–32. In both sections the pagan spiral into darkness begins with *hardness of heart* which leads to *distorted thinking* which in turn brings *alienation from God,* out of which flows a *consuming sensuality.*

the futility of their thinking. Paul emphasizes the connection between thought and behavior. By means of three phrases he hammers home his point that Gentiles live as they do because their thinking is amiss. He points to "the futility of their thinking," to the fact that "they are darkened in their understanding" and to their "ignorance." Right thinking does matter if a person is to get on with right living.

4:18 *hardening of their hearts.* The center of their being (the heart) has become "stonelike" or "petrified." The word Paul uses is *poros* and it means "marble" or a "callus."

4:19 *sensuality / impurity / lust.* By these three nouns Paul describes what the pagan lifestyle had evolved into. Such forms of over-indulgence (lack of self-control) stand in contrast to the "sensitivity" which ought to characterize life.

4:20–21 *to know Christ / heard of him / taught in him.* In contrast to the three phrases which describe the wrong thinking of the pagan, Paul sets these three phrases which describe how the Christian comes to learn the right way of thinking. The first phrase, "to know Christ" is literally "to learn the Messiah" and focuses on the fact that Christ is the subject matter of their education. The second phrase, "you heard of him" is literally "you heard him" and emphasizes that Jesus is the teacher. The third phrase, "you were taught in him" makes the point that Jesus is the very environment within which their learning takes place. The path to right thinking (and hence to right living) is via the school of the Messiah.

4:22–24 *put off / put on.* Paul develops a clothing metaphor here. At conversion, the Christian sheds (strips off) his or her old, ragged, filthy garment and puts on a fresh, new cloak.

old self / new self. "Every time the singular of the 'man' (self) occurs in Ephesians the 'man' mentioned has a specific relation to Christ. The 'perfect man' (4:13) as well as the 'inner man' (3:16–17) is Christ himself. Therefore, in 4:24 the 'new man' (new self) is most likely Christ himself, the 'old man' (old self) is Adam, the anti-type of Christ (Rom. 5:12–21; 1 Cor. 15:21–28,45–55)" (Barth). In conversion, therefore, the Christian puts off his or her old, sinful nature and puts on the very life of Christ himself.

4:23 *be made new.* The verbs translated "put off" and "put on" are in the aorist tense, that is, they signify a completed past action. This exchange of natures occurs at conversion. Here the verb tense is a present infinitive, "be made new" or "be renewed," indicating the need for ongoing, continual renewal. Once again Paul is saying, "Be what you are."

the attitude of your minds. Again, the emphasis is on right thinking in order to be able to live right.

4:25–32 Paul now gives a few concrete examples of what this new lifestyle looks like. It is characterized by truth (v. 25), by proper control of anger (vv. 26–27), by honest labor (v. 28), by edifying talk (vv. 29–30), by love (vv. 31–32).

4:25 *Therefore.* Having just described what is indeed so for Christians (they have a new self which bears the marks of God's very nature: righteousness and holiness), Paul will now describe specifically what their lifestyle ought to be. This verse is a model for how Paul discusses each of the six topics. He begins with the negative deed, in this case, falsehood. (In Greek the word is literally "the lie.") Then he sets in contrast the positive virtue which he commends, in this case, truthful speech. Then he gives a reason for this command. Here it is that we are all neighbors. In fact, we are even closer than that, "we are all members of one body." Lies destroy fellowship. Unity must be built on trust and trust comes via truth.

4:26 *In your anger.* Paul recognizes that there is such a thing as legitimate anger. Paul says in 5:6 that God experiences anger, though the translation obscures this meaning. (Although the phrase in 5:6 is rendered as "God's wrath," the same word is used there which is here translated "anger.") Jesus was angry (Mark 3:5). There are certain situations in which anger is the only honest response. For Christians to deny their anger is dangerous and self-defeating. But once admitted, anger is to be dealt with and so Paul identifies four ways to deal with anger. First, "in your anger do not sin." What is the source of the anger? Is it wounded pride or real wrong? Is it spite or is it injustice? In verse 31 Paul will point out that "rage and anger" are to be gotten rid of. Second, "Do not let the sun go down" on your anger, that is, deal with it quickly. Do not nurse anger and let it grow. Third, do not let anger develop into resentment. This is what the word translated "angry" at the end of verse 26 means. Get the anger out in the open. Be reconciled if possible. Apologize if necessary. Fourth, "do not give the devil a foothold." Do not let Satan exploit your anger, turning it into hostility or using it to disrupt fellowship.

4:28 It is not enough simply to stop stealing, the thief must also start working.

4:29–30 From the use of one's hands, Paul turns to the use of one's mouth. The word translated "unwholesome" means "rotten" and is used to describe spoiled fruit (as in Matt. 12:33). Instead of rancid words that wound others, the words of Christians ought to edify ("building others up"), be appropriate ("according to their needs"), bring grace (this is the literal rendering of the word translated "benefit"), and not cause distress for the Holy Spirit (by unholy words).

4:31 Paul identifies six negative attitudes which must be erased from the Christian life.

bitterness. Spiteful, long-standing resentment.

rage and anger. These two attitudes are related. The first is a more immediate flare-up while the latter is a more long-term, sullen hostility. This is not the "righteous anger" Paul dealt with in verse 26.

brawling. Loud self-assertion; screaming arguments.

slander. Insulting someone else behind his or her back.

malice. Wishing or plotting evil against another.

4:32 In contrast to the negative attitudes listed in verse 31, here Paul identifies a set of positive attitudes that ought to characterize the Christian. Instead of bitterness, rage, anger, brawling, slander, and malice the Christian is to display kindness, compassion and forgiveness.

UNIT 10—Children of Light—Part 2 / Eph. 5:1-21

5 Be imitators of God, therefore, as dearly loved children ²and live a life of love, just as Christ loved us and gave himself up for us as a fragrant offering and sacrifice to God.

³But among you there must not be even a hint of sexual immorality, or of any kind of impurity, or of greed, because these are improper for God's holy people. ⁴Nor should there be obscenity, foolish talk or coarse joking, which are out of place, but rather thanksgiving. ⁵For of this you can be sure: No immoral, impure or greedy person—such a man is an idolater—has any inheritance in the kingdom of Christ and of God.ᵃ ⁶Let no one deceive you with empty words, for because of such things God's wrath comes on those who are disobedient. ⁷Therefore do not be partners with them.

⁸For you were once darkness, but now you are light in the Lord. Live as children of light ⁹(for the fruit of the light consists in all goodness, righteousness and truth) ¹⁰and find out what pleases the Lord. ¹¹Have nothing to do with the fruitless deeds of darkness, but rather expose them. ¹²For it is shameful even to men-tion what the disobedient do in secret. ¹³But everything exposed by the light becomes visible, ¹⁴for it is light that makes everything visible. This is why it is said:

> "Wake up, O sleeper,
>   rise from the dead,
>   and Christ will shine on you."

¹⁵Be very careful, then, how you live—not as unwise but as wise, ¹⁶making the most of every opportunity, because the days are evil. ¹⁷Therefore do not be foolish, but understand what the Lord's will is. ¹⁸Do not get drunk on wine, which leads to debauchery. Instead, be filled with the Spirit. ¹⁹Speak to one another with psalms, hymns and spiritual songs. Sing and make music in your heart to the Lord, ²⁰always giving thanks to God the Father for everything, in the name of our Lord Jesus Christ.

²¹Submit to one another out of reverence for Christ.

ᵃ5 Or *kingdom of the Christ and God*

READ

First Reading / First Impressions: How do you think this passage would be received today in a locker room?

Second Reading / Big Idea: If you were a "Reader's Digest" editor assigned to pare this down to two or three verses, which would you choose?

SEARCH

1. What models for our new life in Christ does Paul give us here?

(v. 1)

(v. 2)

2. How do these models automatically rule out the behaviors Paul rejects in verses 3–5?

3. What type of false teaching must have been going on for Paul to issue the warning of verses 5–6?

4. From verses 7 and 11, what are some implications for how Christians ought to relate to those who teach that the behaviors of verses 5–6 are all right?

5. What additional models of the Christian life does Paul give in verses 8b and 15?

(v. 8b)

(v. 15)

6. Based on these models, what are we to do and not do as Christians according to verses 9–18?

TO DO

TO NOT DO

7. From verses 18–21, what qualities characterize the "Spirit-filled" life (see notes on these verses)?

APPLY

Paul uses the Trinity as the model for our lifestyle as Christians. Consider how you might specifically put into practice each of these models. One specific way I want to imitate my heavenly Father now is:

I want to follow the Son's model of sacrificial love by (think of one way to care for a specific person or situation):

Of the qualities of joy, thankfulness and submission marking life in the Spirit, I most need to practice:

GROUP AGENDA

After the first part, read the Scripture out loud and divide into groups of 4. Then come back together for the third part.

TO BEGIN / 10–15 Min. (Choose 1 or 2)

1. Did you ever have your mouth washed out with soap? What other method did your parents use for "cleaning up" your language?

2. What is the worst practical joke you have played on someone or someone has played on you?

3. As a child, what is one thing about your parents you remember trying to copy?

TO GO DEEPER / 30 Min. (Choose 2 or 3)

1. If you have completed the homework, what stands out the most to you in READ or SEARCH?

2. What is the difference between "foolish talk or coarse joking" (v. 4) and a good belly laugh? Between the "fruitless deeds of darkness" (v. 11) and good clean fun?

3. When have you felt pressured to go along with the crowd even when you knew it wasn't right? What have you found helpful in resisting pressure to do something you shouldn't?

4. What have you learned in this passage and the notes about being "filled with the Spirit"?

5. CASE STUDY: Johnny was a fun person to be around. Then, he got a good case of "religion." He has dropped his old friends and spends most of his time studying the Bible. When he sees his old friends, he scolds them or "preaches" at them. If you were Johnny's friend, how would you deal with him?

TO CLOSE / 15–30 Min.

1. How are you doing on your group mission?

2. Share your answer to one of the questions in APPLY.

3. Of all the "do's" and "don'ts" of this passage, which one have you seen the most growth in? Which one do you most need to grow in?

4. How can the group pray for you?

NOTES

Summary. Paul continues his commentary on what the Christian lifestyle ought to look like in contrast to the pagan lifestyle that so many of them lived out prior to coming to faith. He begins by urging the imitation of God by living a life of love (5:1–2) in contrast to the life of lust they once knew (5:3–4). Then he moves to the whole question of incentives. Why should a person live a life in imitation of God? In 5:5–21 Paul identifies four incentives for Christian living.

5:1–2 If the Ephesians want to know what the Christian lifestyle is all about, they simply have to look at how God lives. They can see this by looking at Jesus who is God-come-in-the-flesh. In Jesus they will see that the divine way is the way of self-giving love. This is the basic model for the Christian life. If one lives in love, then all the specific behaviors Paul has been pointing out will flow naturally.

5:3–4 From love, Paul turns to lust. In these verses, in contrast to the Christian way which he just described, he defines the pagan way which they might be tempted to follow. Christians must not give in to sexual immorality, even though among Gentiles in the first century such behavior was rampant. In Athens, for example, a Temple to Aphrodite, the goddess of love, was built with the profits of prostitution. In Corinth, many of the temples were run by priestesses who were, in fact, sacred prostitutes. Cicero argued with great eloquence that young men should be allowed to visit prostitutes. It was the norm in those days for a man to have a mistress. With these verses, Paul completes his list of six specific sets of behaviors—given in negative and then positive form—which ought to characterize the life of the Christian. First, he said: Don't lie but instead tell the truth (4:25). Second: Don't let your anger lead to sin but instead deal with it (4:26–27). Third: Don't steal but instead work and be generous to the needy (4:28). Fourth: Don't speak in an unwholesome way but instead use your speech to edify (4:29–30). Fifth: Don't be bitter and unkind but instead be compassionate and loving (4:31–5:2). Sixth: Don't be obscene about sex but instead be thankful for it (5:3–4).

5:3 *sexual immorality / impurity.* These two words (*porneia* or fornication and *akatharsia* or uncleanness) cover all forms of promiscuous sexual behavior among married or unmarried people.

greed. Literally "insatiability."

not be even a hint. Even naming such sins (in word or thought) is harmful.

5:4 Vulgar talk is out of place because it demeans God's good gift of sex which is a subject for thanksgiving and not joking.

5:5–21 Paul's subject in verse 5 is still overindulgence, but he has moved into a new phase of his argument. Having just identified six specific sets of behavior which ought to characterize Christians, now he will point out four incentives to proper living. Paul has moved from model to motive. The four incentives are the fact of judgment (vv. 5–7), the implications of being a child of light (vv. 8–14), the nature of wisdom (vv. 15–17), and the filling of the Holy Spirit (vv. 18–21).

5:5–7 Judgment is real. Those who live, without repentance, a committed, public life of self-indulgent sensuality will be called to account. The warning here is that "if we should fall into a life of greedy immorality, we would be supplying clear evidence that we are after all idolators, not worshipers of God and so heirs not of heaven, but of hell" (Stott).

5:5 *greedy person.* The reference is to the sexually greedy person.

idolater. When vice has become an obsession, it functions in a person's life as a "god" (or idol), drawing forth passionate commitment of time and energy.

5:6 *empty words.* The Gnostics taught (wrongly) that sins of the body did not matter and would not taint the soul.

5:8–14 A second reason why Christians should not get involved in immoral practices (v. 11) is that they have become "children of light" (v. 8). In fact, it is not just that they walk in the light, they "are light in the Lord" (v. 8). To be such a child of light implies a lifestyle of "goodness, righteousness and truth" (v. 9).

5:8 *darkness / light.* Darkness represents that which is secret and evil and is out of touch with God's purposes. Light stands for goodness and truth, and for open obedience to God.

5:9 *fruit of the light.* Paul defines these as "goodness" which is a generosity of spirit that comes of doing God's will, "righteousness" which is just actions toward others, and "truth" which is honest dealings with others.

5:11 In contrast to "the fruit of the light" are "fruitless deeds of darkness." The Christian's response to "deeds of darkness" is, on the negative side, to "have nothing to do" with them. On the positive side, the Christian is to "expose" these deeds. The effect of light will be to reveal the ugliness of sin.

5:14a J.B. Phillips translates this verse, "It is even possible ... for light to turn the thing it shines upon into light also."

5:14b This is probably a quotation from an ancient Christian hymn. "Conversion is nothing less than awakening out of sleep, rising from death and being brought out of darkness into the light of Christ" (Stott).

5:15–17 A third impulse to Christian living is wisdom. Paul assumes that wisdom will teach one how to live (i.e. wisdom is practical and not merely theoretical); and that it is better to be wise than a fool.

5:18–21 Paul's final motive for Christian living is that such is the outcome when one is filled with the Holy Spirit. Grammatically, Paul begins this section with two imperative statements or commands. *Do not get drunk,* rather *be filled* with the Holy Spirit; followed by four present participles which define the result of the Spirit's infilling: speaking, singing, thanking and submitting (Stott).

5:18 *drunk.* Be filled with the Spirit not with "spirits"!

be filled. This is a command, not an option. It is issued to all Christians (in Greek, it is plural). The present tense of the verb signifies continuous action ("go on being filled") and since the command is in the passive voice it means "let the Spirit fill you" as the New English Bible renders the phrase.

5:19 Public worship is in view here and the aim is mutual edification.

5:20 *giving thanks ... for everything.* The "everything" for which thanks is offered is "everything" which is consistent with who God is as the qualifiers indicate: give thanks to God, in the name of Jesus. To give thanks for cancer or adultery is to praise God for evil, which cannot flow out of his nature. (That God can turn evil to good is quite another matter.)

5:21 *submit to one another.* The fourth aspect of being filled with the Spirit involves mutual submission within the Christian community. The NIV begins a new paragraph and new unit at verse 22. In fact, verse 21 both concludes the previous unit (vv. 18–20) and begins the new unit (vv. 22–24) since it supplies the final participle for 5:18 as well as the verb for 5:22.

UNIT 11—Wives & Husbands / Ephesians 5:22–33

Wives and Husbands

²²Wives, submit to your husbands as to the Lord. ²³For the husband is the head of the wife as Christ is the head of the church, his body, of which he is the Savior. ²⁴Now as the church submits to Christ, so also wives should submit to their husbands in everything.

*²⁵Husbands, love your wives, just as Christ loved the church and gave himself up for her ²⁶to make her holy, cleansing*ᵃ her by the washing with water through the word, ²⁷and to present her to himself as a radiant church, without stain or wrinkle or any other blemish, but holy and blameless. ²⁸In this same way, husbands ought to love their wives as their own bodies. He who loves his wife loves himself. ²⁹After all, no one ever hated his own body, but he feeds and cares for it, just as Christ does the church—³⁰for we are members of his body. ³¹"For this reason a man will leave his father and mother and be united to his wife, and the two will become one flesh."ᵇ ³²This is a profound mystery—but I am talking about Christ and the church. ³³However, each one of you also must love his wife as he loves himself, and the wife must respect her husband.*

ᵃ26 Or *having cleansed*   ᵇ31 Gen. 2:24

READ

First Reading / First Impressions: My first reaction to this passage is:
- ❏ Paul would be blown to bits by feminists.
- ❏ It would be nice if this was the way things worked, but ...
- ❏ My spouse needs to read this.
- ❏ I need to read this.

Second Reading / Big Idea: What are three or four key words in this passage?

SEARCH

1. Given 5:3–5, what attitudes about sex and marriage might Paul have to combat?

2. In the Greek, verse 22 is a clause "borrowing" the verb from verse 21 (see notes on v. 22). Given the problems involved in 5:3–5, why might Paul apply the general principle of verse 21 to the wife?

3. What motives does he give (vv. 23–24; see notes on v. 23 as well)?

4. Again, given 5:3–5, why does Paul address husbands the way he does (v. 25)?

5. What specifically does Paul say is involved in this type of love (vv. 25b–30)?

(v. 25)

(vv. 26–27)

(vv. 28–30)

6. How is the call to the husbands an application of the general principle of 5:21?

7. In your own words, express the goal of Christian marriage in verse 31.

APPLY
If you are married, go back over the Scripture passage for specific instructions for your part and role in the marriage bond. In the left column, jot down what they are. In the right column, write one thing you could do to carry out each of the instructions in the next few days.

WHAT I AM SUPPOSED TO DO	WHAT I AM GOING TO DO ABOUT IT

If you are single, what are your feelings about marriage? What is the message of this passage for you?

GROUP AGENDA

After the first part, read the Scripture out loud and divide into groups of 4. Then come back together for the third part.

TO BEGIN / 10–15 Min. (Choose 1 or 2)

1. Who was your first "true love"?

2. What is the funniest thing that happened at your wedding or honeymoon?

3. What couple do you admire as a good role model for marriage?

TO GO DEEPER / 30 Min. (Choose 2 or 3)

1. In the culture of his day, would Paul be considered more of a "male chauvinist" or a "radical feminist"?

2. What have you learned from the homework and the notes about "submission" in marriage?

3. Which role, wife or husband, do you think is more difficult?

4. What should a wife do when her husband does not take spiritual leadership?

5. (Husbands) How seriously do you take the spiritual nurture of your wife?

6. (Wives) What are you doing to encourage your husband in his responsibility?

7. CASE STUDY: John and Mary met and married in college. Both came from "traditional" homes where the husband was "boss" and the wife was the "submissive" partner. Lately, they have been struggling both in their marriage and their spiritual lives. They come to you for help in the way you would work through the "role" problem.

TO CLOSE / 15–30 Min.

1. How did your group answer the three "Brainstorming" questions on page M19 in the center section?

2. Share your answer in the APPLY section.

3. What prayer needs do you have for the group?

NOTES

Summary. In discussing what is involved in living the Christian life, Paul has so far pointed out the need for unity (within the church) and the need for purity (within the individual). In 5:22–6:9 he turns to a third subject: the need for quality relationships at home and work. These three sets of relationships—within marriage, across generations, and in the workplace—form the core of most people's lives and it is crucial that they be lived out in accord with the will of Christ if a Christian is to be all he or she can be.

5:22 The verb in 5:21 ("submit") is linked grammatically both backward to 5:18 and forward to this verse. Looking backward, "submit" is the last of four present participles which describe what is involved in being filled with the Spirit. Looking forward, "submit" provides the verb for this verse which has no verb of its own.

Wives. Paul first spells out what "mutual submission" means for wives. In a radical departure from tradition, Paul addresses women in their own right as individuals able to make their own choices. He does not address them through their husbands (as would have been common in the first century). He does not tell husbands: "Make your wives submit to you." He speaks to wives on the same level as he will next speak to husbands.

submit. This injunction from Paul must be understood in its historical context. In Jewish law a woman was a "thing," not a person, and she had no legal rights. In describing the Greek world, Demosthenes wrote: "We have courtesans for our pleasure, prostitutes for daily physical use, wives to bring up legitimate children." In Rome, too, divorce was easy and women were repressed. Against this Paul proposes a radical, liberating view: (1) submission was to be mutual (the man was no longer the absolute authority); (2) wives are called upon to defer only to their husbands (and not all women to all men); and (3) submission is defined and qualified by Christ's headship of the church (Christ died for the church). Therefore what it is that wives are called to submit to ("yield to," "adapt to," or "give way to") is sacrificial love! Love, not control, is the issue.

5:23 as. The reason why wives should submit to husbands is given by means of a simile (that is, a direct comparison of one thing with another introduced by "like," "as," or "so").

Christ is the head of the church. Paul has already described in 4:15–16 the way in which Christ is the head of the church. He is head in that the rest of the body derives from him the health and strength which allows each part to play its own distinctive role. It is a headship of love, not of control; of nurture, not of suppression. The word "head" when used today has the sense of "ruler" or "authority." However, in Greek when "head" is used in a metaphorical sense as it is here, it means "origin" as in the "source (head) of a river." Woman has her origins in man (see Gen. 2:18–23) just as the church has its origins in Christ. Had Paul wanted to convey the idea that the husband "rules over" the wife (as Christ "rules over" the church) he would have used a different Greek word for "head."

the Savior. The emphasis in this analogy is not on Christ as Lord but on Christ as Savior. Paul is not saying husbands are to express "headship" via the exertion of some sort of authority (as befits a "lord") but via the expression of sacrificial love (as characterized by the Savior).

5:25–33 Having addressed the role of wives in three verses, Paul now devotes nine verses to the role of husbands! Nowhere in these verses does Paul define the husband's role in terms of authority over his wife. In fact the word authority (*exousia*) is not used once in 5:22–6:9.

5:25 *love your wives.* This is the main thing Paul says to husbands. It is so important that he repeats this injunction three times (vv. 25,28,33). Love is what the husband gives by way of his part in the mutual submission paradigm. This attitude stands in contrast to Jewish teaching. "The rabbis asserted that money, the contract, and intercourse make marriage. When they enumerated what else a man 'owed' to his wife, they seldom mentioned love" (Barth). As for Greek culture, although certain philosophers such as Aristotle taught that men ought to love their wives, they used a mild word for love (*phileo*) signifying the sort of affection a person has for family. Here, however, Paul urges a far stronger type of love: *agape,* which is characterized by sacrificial, self-giving action.

just as Christ loved the church and gave himself up for her. Paul now makes quite clear in what sense he is speaking of Christ as head over the church. Two actions characterize Christ's role for the church: love and sacrifice. The husband is called upon to act toward his wife in the same way, that is, to die for her! (This is how Christ "gave himself up for the church.")

5:25–27 In comparing the marriage relationship to the relationship between Christ and the church, Paul is following a long tradition in Scripture. The Old Testament often pictured God's relationship to his people in terms of a marriage covenant (Isa. 54:4–6; Jer. 2:1–3; 31:31–32; Hos. 1:3). In the New Testament, Christ is seen as the bridegroom (Mark 2:19–20; John 3:29).

5:26 *the washing with water.* The reference is to the bridal bath prior to the wedding that was the custom of both Jews and Greeks. The action in view here is Christian baptism.

through the word. This refers either to the confession of faith by the baptismal candidate or to the preaching of the Gospel that evoked the faith initially.

5:27 *to present her.* At a Jewish wedding the bride was presented to the groom by a friend. This was understood as a sacred duty because it was first performed by God when he brought Eve to Adam (Gen. 2:22). In this case, Jesus is both he who presents and he who receives the bride.

radiant. The word in Greek is *endoxos* and can also be translated "resplendent" or "glorious." On one level it refers to the beautiful garments worn by the bride. On another level, this word is derived from *doxa,* which refers to the very radiance of God. The church, his bride, has about her the aura of God.

without stain or wrinkle. The bridegroom has removed any trace of disease (pox marks or leprosy), disfigurement or neglect.

5:28–31 In describing how husbands are to love their wives, Paul turns from the exalted vision of Christ's love for the church to the more mundane (but eminently realistic) level of the husband's love for himself!

5:31 *one flesh.* Paul does not view marriage as some sort of spiritual covenant devoid of sexuality. His second illustration of how a husband is to love his wife (vv. 28–31) revolves around their sexual union, as made explicit by his quotation of Genesis 2:24.

5:33 *as he loves himself.* In Leviticus 19:18, the Israelites are called upon to "love your neighbor as yourself." The gauge by which they will know if they are loving others properly is self-love. "Is this how I want to be loved?" Husbands, according to Paul, can use this same gauge for measuring their love for their wives.

respect. When a husband loves his wife in this way he will receive, in return, respect.

UNIT 12—Children & Parents / Slaves & Masters / Eph. 6:1-9

Children and Parents

6 Children, obey your parents in the Lord, for
this is right. ²"Honor your father and mother"—which is the first commandment with a
promise—³"that it may go well with you and that
you may enjoy long life on the earth."ª

⁴Fathers, do not exasperate your children;
instead, bring them up in the training and
instruction of the Lord.

Slaves and Masters

⁵Slaves, obey your earthly masters with
respect and fear, and with sincerity of heart, just
as you would obey Christ. ⁶Obey them not only
to win their favor when their eye is on you, but
like slaves of Christ, doing the will of God from
your heart. ⁷Serve wholeheartedly, as if you were
serving the Lord, not men, ⁸because you know
that the Lord will reward everyone for whatever
good he does, whether he is slave or free.

⁹And masters, treat your slaves in the same
way. Do not threaten them, since you know that
he who is both their Master and yours is in heav-
en, and there is no favoritism with him.

ª3 Deut. 5:16

READ
First Reading / First Impressions:
If Paul wrote a "Dear Abby" advice column in his day, how popular do you think this advice would be?

Second Reading / Big Idea:
The thing I like about this passage is:

What bothers me about this passage is:

SEARCH
1. What are children commanded to do (v. 1)?

2. What does Paul mean about not exasperating children (see note on v. 4)?

3. What are some ways a parent might bring up their child in the "training and instruction of the Lord"?

4. What qualities do you think would characterize a home where verses 1–4 were really practiced?

5. How is the slave's union with Christ to affect his or her relationship with the master (vv. 5–8; see notes)?

6. In turn, how is the master's union with Christ to affect his relationship with the slaves (v. 9)?

7. How does this whole passage relate to 5:21?

APPLY
Choose one of the four roles in this passage that fits your situation right now: (a) child, (b) parent, (c) slave (employee) or (d) master (employer). Then, do a little "wishing" regarding this role. In the left column, jot down two "wishes" you would like to make for your situation, such as: "I wish I could improve the communication with my teenage daughter," etc. Then in the right column, pick one of the two wishes you jotted down and make two specific steps to work toward the wish, such as: "I'll take my daughter out on a date once a week for six weeks," etc.

TWO WISHES:

TWO STEPS:

5:(21) "Submit to one another out of reverence for Christ."

GROUP AGENDA

After the first part, read the Scripture out loud and divide into groups of 4. Then come back together for the third part.

TO BEGIN / 10–15 Min. (Choose 1 or 2)
1. When you were growing up, what caused the most tension between you and your parents?

2. Who is your favorite TV family? Why?

3. What was your first job? How much money did you make?

4. Who is the best boss you've ever had?

TO GO DEEPER / 30 Min. (Choose 2 or 3)
1. What stands out to you from the homework and the notes about parent/child and master/slave relationships?

✓ 2. What is the difference between "exasperating" your children and practicing "tough love"?

✓ 3. Where do you draw the line between giving your children (or employees) freedom and limits?

✓ 4. In work environments today, what principles in verses 5–9 could help improve employer/employee relationships? What is one you could work on?

5. What do you appreciate most about the way you were brought up? If you have children (now or in the future), what would you like to pass on to them from your own upbringing?

6. CASE STUDY: One of your children is "passive-aggressive"—passive at school and aggressive at home. Her homework is neglected, and if you ask about it, she gets hostile ... and if she "fails," she insists "it's your fault." What do you do?

TO CLOSE / 15–30 Min.
1. Are you planning a kickoff for starting a new small group? Have you made plans for celebrating your time together as a group?

2. What did you jot down under APPLY?

3. How can the group support you in prayer?

NOTES

Summary. Paul continues his discussion of the three basic sets of relationships which dominate most people's lives. Here he deals with relationships within a family between parents and children and the relationship between slaves and masters. Paul begins by urging children to "obey," and then gives four reasons for such obedience: (1) they are "in the Lord"; (2) it is the "right" thing to do; (3) God commands obedience; and (4) obedience brings a rich reward. Parents are then urged to limit the exercise of their authority and to train their children in the ways of the Lord. To slaves Paul says, in essence, "Come to view your work as service to Christ, and thus labor for your master in the same way that you would labor for the Lord." To masters Paul says, in essence, "The slave is a person like you are who is to be treated as you expect to be treated since before God you are both equal."

6:1–3 Paul does not simply command obedience on the part of children. He gives reasons for it. In the same way that he addressed husbands and wives and gave each a rationale for their behavior, he also does the same for children.

6:1 *Children.* The very fact that Paul even addresses children is amazing. Normally all such instructions would come via their parents. That he addresses children in this public letter means that children were in attendance with their families at worship when such a letter would have been read. Paul does not define a "child" here; i.e., he does not deal with the question of when a child becomes an adult and thus ceases to be under parental authority. This is not a real problem, however, since each culture has its own definition of when adulthood begins. Even as adults, however, children are expected to "honor" their parents.

obey. Paul tells children to "obey" ("follow," "be subject to," "listen to"). He uses a different word from that used when speaking of the relationship between wives and husbands. Parents have authority over their children but not husbands over wives. Also, although "obey" is a stronger word than "submit," it is not without limits.

in the Lord. This is the first reason children are to obey their parents. There are two ways in which this phrase can be taken: obey your parents because you are a Christian and/or obey your parents in everything that is compatible with your commitment to Christ.

for this is right. This is the second of the four reasons Paul gives for obedience. "Children obey parents. That is simply the way it is," Paul says. It is not just Christian ethics; it is standard behavior in any society.

6:2 "Honor your father and mother." Paul begins to quote the fifth commandment. This is the third reason children should obey parents. God commands it. "To honor father and mother means more than to obey them, especially if this obedience is interpreted in a merely outward sense. ... To honor implies to love, to regard highly, to show the spirit of respect and consideration" (Hendriksen).

the first commandment with a promise. Paul probably means "first in importance" since the second commandment (Ex. 20:4–6) promises God's love to those who love God.

6:3 This is the fourth reason for obedience. It produces good rewards. Paul identifies the two aspects of the promise. It involved material well-being and long life. The promise is probably not for individual children but for the community of which they are a part. It will be prosperous and long-standing.

6:4 Just as children have a duty to obey, parents have the duty to instruct children with gentleness and restraint.

Fathers. The model for a father is that of God the "Father of all" (4:6). This view of fatherhood stands in sharp contrast to the harsh Roman father who had the power of life and death over his children.

exasperate. Parents are to be responsible for not provoking hostility on the part of their children. By humiliating children, being cruel to them, overindulging them, or being unreasonable, parents squash children rather than encourage them.

bring them up. This verb is to "nourish" or "feed" them.

training. This word can be translated "discipline" and "is training with the accent on the correction of the young" (Houlden).

instruction. The emphasis here is on what is said verbally to children.

6:5–8 That Paul should even address slaves is amazing. In the first century, they were often considered more akin to farm animals than human beings, the only difference being they could talk. Slaves were "living tools" according to Aristotle.

Paul speaks to them as people able to choose and decide—quite revolutionary for his era.

6:5 obey. Paul is not counseling rebellion (an impossibility, in any case, given the conditions of the first century and a cause which could lead only to massive bloodshed). He tells slaves to "obey" and to do so "with respect and fear." He tells them to "serve." The word "obey" is the same one which Paul used to define the child's duty to the parent.

earthly. As opposed to "heavenly." Paul reminds slaves that although at the moment they may be "owned" by another human being, ultimately they belong to Christ who is their true Lord.

with sincerity of heart. Or "with singleness of heart." Paul calls for service to be given with integrity. Slaves are to give their masters the same wholehearted devotion they would give the Lord.

Christ. In each of the four verses addressed to slaves, Christ is mentioned.

6:6 not only to win their favor when their eye is on you. This is a good rendering of the phrase which reads literally, "not by way of eye-service as men-pleasers." In other words, don't just pretend to be serving wholeheartedly when, in fact, you only work when you are watched.

6:8 reward. The life of many slaves was hard and bleak, and there was little hope that it would change (unless perhaps the master got converted and took seriously the Christian message). In this context the hope of future reward was not trivial, but of central importance.

everyone. Paul reminds slaves that before God they stand as on equal footing with their masters.

6:9 treat your slaves in the same way. Paul applies the golden rule to slave owners: to get service and respect, give it to slaves! This was a revolutionary concept. This was the way of mutual submission for slave and master; i.e., mutual respect.

Do not threaten them. In the same way that parents are not to exasperate children, masters are not to browbeat slaves. Punishment was the usual way of controlling slaves. Paul says, "Don't even use threats against the powerless."

no favoritism. The seeds of emancipation are sown here. Paul is pointing out the basic equality in the sight of God between slave and master (see also v. 8).

UNIT 13—Armor of God / Final Greetings / Eph. 6:10-24

The Armor of God

¹⁰Finally, be strong in the Lord and in his mighty power. ¹¹Put on the full armor of God so that you can take your stand against the devil's schemes. ¹²For our struggle is not against flesh and blood, but against the rulers, against the authorities, against the powers of this dark world and against the spiritual forces of evil in the heavenly realms. ¹³Therefore put on the full armor of God, so that when the day of evil comes, you may be able to stand your ground, and after you have done everything, to stand. ¹⁴Stand firm then, with the belt of truth buckled around your waist, with the breastplate of righteousness in place, ¹⁵and with your feet fitted with the readiness that comes from the gospel of peace. ¹⁶In addition to all this, take up the shield of faith, with which you can extinguish all the flaming arrows of the evil one. ¹⁷Take the helmet of salvation and the sword of the Spirit, which is the word of God. ¹⁸And pray in the Spirit on all occasions with all kinds of prayers and requests. With this in mind, be alert and always keep on praying for all the saints.

¹⁹Pray also for me, that whenever I open my mouth, words may be given me so that I will fearlessly make known the mystery of the gospel, ²⁰for which I am an ambassador in chains. Pray that I may declare it fearlessly, as I should.

Final Greetings

²¹Tychicus, the dear brother and faithful servant in the Lord, will tell you everything, so that you also may know how I am and what I am doing. ²²I am sending him to you for this very purpose, that you may know how we are, and that he may encourage you.

²³Peace to the brothers, and love with faith from God the Father and the Lord Jesus Christ. ²⁴Grace to all who love our Lord Jesus Christ with an undying love.

READ

First Reading / First Impressions: Reading Paul's dramatic imagery here makes me feel like ...

❏ the Christian life is more than I thought. ❏ Paul imagines demons under every tree.

❏ it's no wonder life is so hard. ❏ no matter what, God will help me.

Second Reading / Big Idea: How might Paul's "marching orders" be summed up in one sentence?

SEARCH

1. From earlier passages (such as 2:1–3; 4:14,17,19,25–31; 5:3–4), what are some of the devil's schemes which Christians encounter?

2. What are the six parts of the Christian armor and what does each mean (vv. 14–17; see notes)?

3. What special prayer does Paul ask for himself (v. 19)?

4. How does prayer fit into this spiritual battle (see notes on v. 18)?

5. In light of Satan's activity and the commands God gives us here, how would you sum up God's part and our part in the fight against evil?

APPLY
Since this is the last unit in this study, take a moment and measure your spiritual progress since start-ing this course. Circle a number from 1 (weak) to 10 (strong) for each category below.

Knowing the will of God for my life:
1   2   3   4   5   6   7   8   9   10

Developing strong spiritual muscles:
1   2   3   4   5   6   7   8   9   10

Sorting out my life priorities:
1   2   3   4   5   6   7   8   9   10

Experiencing God's grace and peace:
1   2   3   4   5   6   7   8   9   10

Being sensitive to other people:
1   2   3   4   5   6   7   8   9   10

Knowing and using my spiritual gifts:
1   2   3   4   5   6   7   8   9   10

GROUP AGENDA

After the first part, read the Scripture out loud and divide into groups of 4. Then come back together for the third part.

TO BEGIN / 10–15 Min. (Choose 1 or 2)

1. What was some of your (or your kids') favorite dress-up costumes?

2. Who in your family enjoys playing computer games?

3. Which war in history has most captured your attention? Why?

TO GO DEEPER / 30 Min. (Choose 2 or 3)

1. What have you learned, or been reminded of, about "spiritual warfare" in this unit?

2. What evidence do you see of the battle in your life? In your church? In your community? In your nation? In the world?

3. What would it mean for you "to stand" in these particular battlefields?

4. What does Paul mean by picturing the Word of God as the one piece of equipment in the armor of the Christian that is for offensive use (for attack)?

5. CASE STUDY: Jim, a college freshman, is thinking he needs to "live a little" in the freedom of his new environment. Church attendance, personal prayer and participation in a campus fellowship are all in a decline. What is your advice to him when he visits you during Christmas break?

TO CLOSE / 15–30 Min.

1. Take time to share your experience together during this course, using the spiritual measurement under APPLY.

2. What have you gained the most from this study of Ephesians? What was the "serendipity" of this course—the unexpected blessing?

3. Have you finalized your plans for the future of your group?

4. How can this group remember you in prayer?

NOTES

Summary. Paul ends his letter where he began it: with a vision of the heavenly realms. However, unlike chapter one where his focus was on God's kingdom, this time his focus is on Satan's realm. In chapter one he was looking ahead to the treasures laid up in heaven for God's children. Here he explains that, prior to that glorious day, the children of God must wrestle with evil principalities and powers. In 6:10–20, Paul instructs Christians in how to resist these dark powers. The transition between the subject matter of 5:21–6:9 (relationships) and the subject matter of 6:10–20 (warfare) feels abrupt. Yet Paul knew he could not talk about the ideal (harmonious relationships) without also discussing the real (spiritual warfare). The Christian does not live in a vacuum. The believer is influenced by the principalities and powers and this will affect his or her relationships (as well as all other areas of life) if care is not taken. This unit is divided into three parts which follow an opening injunction to "be strong in the Lord" (v. 10). In verses 11–13, Paul defines the enemy and the basic Christian posture toward him. In verses 14–17, he catalogues six pieces of armor vital for success in this battle. In verses 18–20, he speaks directly (i.e. not by metaphor) about the power of prayer in all this.

6:10 *be strong ... in his mighty power.* In order to wage successful warfare against Satan, the Christian must draw upon God's own power. This is not a natural power generated by the Christian.

6:11–12 Paul defines the Christian's opponent in this spiritual warfare. He is crafty ("the devil's schemes"). He is powerful ("the powers of this dark world"). And he is wicked ("the forces of evil"). In other words, the devil is a real opponent and his legions are not to be taken lightly.

6:11 *Put on.* It is not enough simply to rely passively on God's power. The Christian must do something. Specifically, he or she must "put on" God's armor.

full armor. Paul uses here the term *panoplia* (from which the English word "panoply" comes) which can be understood as the complete catalogue of equipment needed by a soldier.

so that you can take your stand. God's armor enables the Christian to stand against Satan.

the devil's schemes. Evil does not operate in the light. It lurks in shadows and strikes unexpectedly with cleverness and subtlety.

6:12 our struggle. The King James Version translates this phrase as "we wrestle," and indeed Paul shifts his metaphor here from the military field to the gymnasium and an athletic contest.

flesh and blood. Human beings. See 1 Corinthians 15:50; Hebrews 2:14.

the rulers / the authorities / the powers / the spiritual forces. By these various titles Paul names the diverse spiritual forces which rage against humanity. These are intangible spiritual entities whose will is often worked out via concrete historical, economic, political, social and institutional structures. Part of the call to Christians is to identify the places where these evil powers are at work. As to the difference between the demons mentioned in the Gospels and the powers identified here, Marcus Barth says that the distinction "appears to be that the demons affect the individual whereas the powers threaten all men at all times." Demons can be dispatched by an exorcist, but to cope with the powers requires the full use of armor of God.

the powers of this dark world. This phrase can be translated as "the world rulers of this darkness." "World rulers" is a term from astrology and refers to a planet-wide reign of those beings who, according to this philosophy, control the fate of the human race. It was no empty boast on Satan's part when during Jesus' temptations he claims to be able to give him "all the kingdoms of the world" (Matt. 4:8; see also John 12:31; 14:30; 16:11; Eph. 2:2; 1 John 5:19). These "world rulers" have real power and even though Christ has defeated them, they refuse to concede their defeat (though at Christ's Second Coming they will be forced to do so).

forces of evil. Another characteristic of these supernatural beings is wickedness. They are of the darkness, not of the light.

6:13 The day of evil. Although Paul may have in mind the final Day of Judgment when Christ returns and the hostile powers are subdued once and for all, the immediate reference is to those times of pressure and testing that come to all Christians, when steadfast resistance of evil is called for and made possible by the full armor of God.

stand your ground. This is the second time Paul has spoken about "standing fast" (see also v. 11). Twice more he will urge the same thing (a second time in v. 13 and in v. 14). This is the basic posture of the Christian in the face of evil: resistance.

"Standing firm" is a military image. Paul may well have in mind the fighting position of the Roman legions. Fully equipped soldiers were virtually impervious to enemy onslaught—unless they panicked and broke ranks. As long as they "stood firm" when the enemy attacked, they would prevail in the long run. Most all of their equipment, as will be seen in verses 14–17, was designed to enable them to "hold the position." This is key to resisting evil. "Wobbly Christians who have no firm foothold in Christ are an easy prey for the devil" (Stott).

6:14–17 Paul describes six pieces of armor in roughly the order in which a Roman soldier would put them on in preparation for battle. All the pieces of armor except one are defensive in nature rather than aggressive in intent. Each piece of armor is then used by Paul as a metaphor for what the Christian needs to stand against the dark forces.

6:14 the belt of truth. The reference is probably to the leather belt on which the Roman soldier hung his sword and by which he secured his tunic and armor so he would be unimpeded in battle. The "truth" referred to is the inner integrity and sincerity by which the Christian fights evil. Lying and deceit are tactics of the enemy.

the breastplate of righteousness. The breastplate (or "mail") was the major piece of armor for the Roman soldier. Made of metal and leather, it protected his vital organs. "Righteousness" refers to the right standing before God that is the status of the Christian out of which moral conduct and character emerges. In the battle against evil, it is vital to have an assured relationship with God as well as the kind of character that stands in sharp contrast to the evil which is being resisted.

6:15 feet fitted. These are leather half-boots worn by the Roman legionnaire, with heavy studded soles that enabled him to dig in and resist being pushed out of place.

readiness. This term can be translated as "firmness" or "steadfastness" in which case the "gospel of peace" is understood to provide the solid foundation on which the Christian stands in the fight against evil.

6:16 the shield of faith. A large, oblong shield constructed of layers of wood on an iron frame, which was then covered with linen and hide. When wet, such a shield could absorb "flaming arrows."

flaming arrows. These were pitch-soaked arrows. Their aim was not so much to kill a soldier as to set him aflame and cause him to break rank and create panic. In terms of the metaphor, "the fiery missiles" to which the saints are exposed are not the pangs of carnal desire or the signs of very special personal afflictions and conflicts, but they are "to be identified as the influences, temptations, tests, persecution and sufferings that came from outside the community of the saints" (Barth).

6:17 the helmet of salvation. A heavy, metal head-covering lined with felt or sponge which gave substantial protection to the soldier's head from all but the heaviest axe blow. Salvation is like that. The sure knowledge that one's salvation is secure—that the outcome of the battle is already known—is the final defense against Satan.

sword. A short, stabbing sword used for personal combat. The sword is the only piece of offensive equipment in the armor. The main task of the Christian is to withstand the onslaught of evil powers, not to attack (Paul is not calling for a holy war in this section, except in one way—by telling forth the word of God in the power of the Spirit. The writer of Hebrews explains how the word of God operates. "For the word of God is living and active. Sharper than any doubled-edged sword, it penetrates even to dividing soul and spirit, joints and marrow; it judges the thoughts and attitudes of the heart" (Heb. 4:12).

6:18 pray. Paul does not appear to consider prayer a seventh weapon. Rather, it underlies the whole process of spiritual warfare.

in the Spirit. The Bible, the Word of God, is the sword of the Spirit. So, too, prayer is guided by the Spirit. This is, after all, spiritual warfare.

all. There is a comprehensiveness and universality to Paul's call to prayer reflected in his four uses of "all" in verse 18. Pray on all occasions; in all ways; always persevering; and for all the saints.

6:19 fearlessly. Twice Paul uses this Word in reference to his preaching. What Paul asks for is "courage, confidence, boldness, fearlessness, especially in the presence of persons of high rank" (Arndt and Gingrich).

6:20 ambassador in chains. Paul was under house arrest. Day and night he was chained to the wrist of one soldier after another. (Perhaps their constant presence was the inspiration for the armor metaphor.)

6:21–24 It now remains only for Paul to say goodbye. His letter is complete. He has said all that is necessary about the new reality created by God (the multinational church) and the new style of life which its members are to live out. The last four verses are more "housekeeping" in nature than content oriented. Paul has two things to say in these verses. First, he commends Tychicus and indicates that he will convey information to them about the state of affairs with Paul. Second, he concludes the letter with the traditional Greek "wish for blessing" though in a nontraditional, Christianized fashion. In fact, by his choice of benediction he sums up the whole book.

6:21 Tychicus. While Paul was in prison he sent his trusted colleague, Tychicus, on a mission to Asia Minor. Tychicus carried with him in this letter.

6:23 Peace. This has been a major theme of his letter. In Part 1, Paul pointed out that Christ has become our peace. He has done this by breaking down the wall that separated Jew and Gentile, thus ending the hostility and bringing peace between them. This peace between people became possible when Jesus made peace between God and humanity by reconciling men and women to God through the cross. Jesus' message was a message of peace (2:14–18). This being the "way things are," Paul could then go on in Part 2 of his epistle and urge the Christian to maintain this bond of peace. As he closes his letter, he asks for this very same peace for them.

love. Likewise, love has been a major theme in Ephesians. The book began with the affirmation that it was in love God predestined us to be his children (1:4–5) and that it was because of his great love for us that he rescued us from our sin (2:4–5). Then in Paul's great prayer by which he ends Part 2 of the epistle, he asks that we be granted insight into this all-encompassing love of God. In the second half of the book, the practical section, not surprisingly, love is central. It is one of the attitudes that generates unity (4:2); speaking "truth in love" brings maturity (4:15–16); and "a life of love" modeled after Christ is how Christians ought to live (5:1–2). Likewise, love is central to Paul's discussion of the relationship between wife and husband (5:22–33).

6:24 Grace. Paul's third request is that they continue to receive God's grace. Grace, too, has been a theme in Ephesians. It is by grace that we have been saved (1:6–7; 2:5–8); it was by grace that Paul was called into ministry (3:7); and it is by grace that each Christian has received gifts of ministry (4:7).